03/05

-2

Artists in Profile

IMPRESSIONISTS

Jeremy Wallis

Heinemann Library
Chicago, Illinois

Designed by Tinstar Design
Originated by Ambassador Litho
Printed by South China Printing Company, Hong Kong / China
07 06 05 04 03
10 9 8 7 6 5 4 3 2 1

Library of Congress Cataloging-in-Publication Data
Wallis, Jeremy.
 Impressionists / Jeremy Wallis.
   p. cm. -- (Artists in profile)
Includes bibliographical references and index.
Summary: Discusses the characteristics of the Impressionism movement
which began in the 1860s and presents biographies of fourteen
Impressionist artists.
 ISBN 1-58810-642-X
 1. Impressionism (Art)--Juvenile literature. 2.
Painters--Biography--Juvenile literature. [1. Impressionism (Art) 2.
Painters.] I. Title. II. Series.
 ND192.I4 W35 2002
 759.05'4--dc21

                    2001005034

Acknowledgments
The author and publishers are grateful to the following for permission to reproduce copyright material:
pp. 5, 10, 12, 13, 17, 35, 36, 37, 45 E. Lessing/Musee D'Orsay, Paris/AKG London; p. 7 E. Lessing/Art Institute,
Chicago/AKG London; p. 8 Private Collection/AKG London; Musee Marmottan, p. 9 Paris/Bridgeman Art Library;
p. 14 Francis G. Mayer/Corbis; p. 15 Philadelphia Museum of Art/Bridgeman Art Library; p. 16 Illustrated London
News Picture Library/Bridgeman Art Library; p. 19 Beaux-Arts, Pau/AKG London; p. 20 Musee d'Orsay/Bridgeman;
pp. 22, 32 National Gallery London, UK/Bridgeman Art Library; p. 23 Hulton Archive; p. 24 Corbis; p. 25 Collection
of the Butler Institute of American Art, Youngstown, Ohio; p. 27 Ny Carlsberg Glyptothek, Copenhagen/AKG
London; p. 29 AKG London; p. 31 Private Collection/Roger- Viollet, Paris/Bridgeman Art Library; p. 39 Private
Collection/Bridgeman Art Library; p. 40 Dreyfus Foundation, Kunstmuseum, Basel, Switzerland/Bridgeman Art Library;
p. 43 Sheldon Memorial Art Gallery, F.M. Hall Collection; p. 47 Nationalmuseum, Stockholm, Sweden/Bridgeman
Art Library; p. 48 Phillips Collection, Washington D.C., USA/Bridgeman Art Library; p. 50 E. G. Buehrle Collection,
Zurich/ AKG London; p. 51 E. Lessing/Musee des Fitzwilliam Museum, University of Cambridge, UK/Bridgeman Art
Library; p. 53 Musee D'Orsay/Bridgeman Art Library.

Cover photograph: *Les Alyscamps* (1888) by Vincent van Gogh/Christie's Images/SuperStock.

Every effort has been made to contact copyright holders of any material reproduced in this book.
Any omissions will be rectified in subsequent printings if notice is given to the publisher.

Some words are shown in bold, **like this.** You can find out what they mean by looking in the glossary.

Contents

What Is Impressionism?

The Impressionists were a group of painters who changed the way artists look at the world and record what they see. Many of them—Paul Cézanne, Edgar Degas, Édouard Manet, Claude Monet, Camille Pissarro, Pierre-Auguste Renoir—are household names. Others are less well-known. Their work is respected and admired today, but a little more than 125 years ago, they were mocked and ridiculed as they started an artistic revolution.

Imagine a world where art schools tell artists how to paint, what to paint, and where to paint. Where having a picture accepted for an art exhibition depends on the artist's willingness to follow strict rules of picture composition, **perspective,** and color. Where only the great and the good—the rich or famous—have their portraits painted, while ordinary people are considered unsuitable as subjects. Imagine a world that believes nature should be romanticized, prettified, or entirely imagined by the artist. This was the situation in nineteenth-century France.

The Impressionists wanted to paint what they saw rather than what the rules said they should paint. This idea of art went against the style of art that was promoted by the **art establishment.** Each Impressionist had his or her own ideas about art, and each differed from the others in technique and subject. Impressionists often disagreed with each other. But they recognized that they had much in common, and gathered together to exhibit their art.

The art establishment in France

For years, France had an official system of teaching and exhibiting art. In Paris alone, there were hundreds of art schools and **ateliers.** No other city had as many places to study art. However, the art establishment believed they knew the best way to paint. They controlled most of the art schools and the major exhibition—the **Salon**—where artists could build their reputation. They used their power to keep new artists in line. Artists who ignored the rules were often prevented from exhibiting.

The Salon

The official system of art education was crowned by the Salon, the annual exhibition organized by the Royal Academy of Painting and Sculpture. The most important artistic event in the country, the Salon made news around the world. Attendance was high. Pieces were chosen by a jury, which caused bitter arguments because of the importance of being accepted. This selection by jury was one reason the Impressionists banded together. They believed the artists themselves should choose the works they wanted to exhibit.

Most aspiring artists enrolled in the studios of established painters. One of the best known studios was that of Charles Gleyre. During his career Gleyre taught more than 600 students, including Renoir, Jean-Frédéric Bazille, Monet, and Alfred Sisley. Gleyre was seen as strange because he valued originality. Bazille later said that thanks to Gleyre "I shall at least be able to boast that I have not copied anybody."

Most artists spent time copying **Old Masters** to understand their techniques. Renoir said, "It is in the museum that one must learn to paint." Manet, Mary Cassatt, and Degas copied there. Only Monet was confident enough in his talent to believe he did not need to study these great works.

The Écoles des Beaux Arts

The Écoles des Beaux Arts (Schools of Fine Art) were official art schools financed and run by the French government. The most famous was the École Nationale Supérieure des Beaux-Arts in Paris, founded in 1648. Many Impressionists attended this school, including Degas, Manet, and Renoir. The conservative teaching methods practiced there increased these artists' frustration with the art establishment.

The Ball at Moulin de la Galette, by Auguste Renoir (1876)
Depicting a regular Sunday dance in Montmartre, Paris, this is one of Renoir's best-known paintings. He knew from his own experiences how hard the working lives of young Parisians were. He liked to show how they could also enjoy themselves.

Art revolution

The Impressionists were revolutionary in several ways. One reason is that their choice of subject was unique. The **art establishment** believed people wanted to see an optimistic version of reality instead of seeing things as they were. The public went along with this. They did not want realistic landscapes; they wanted to see perfect clouds, perfect trees, and beautiful buildings. In portraits, the public wanted to see famous people, heroes, and people of flawless beauty. They did not want to own pictures of people they would not allow into their homes.

However, realism attracted many painters, writers, and poets. These artists were living in times of incredible scientific, social, and industrial change. They were both fascinated with and frightened by these changes. Industrialization altered the French landscape with railroad bridges, tracks, factories, and new towns. The Impressionists wanted to record these changes. Some Impressionists were interested in people, especially the new urban classes—people who lived and worked in modern towns. They recorded the fun in modern people's lives: festivals and dances, the circus, the music hall, and the ballet. Other artists, including the female Impressionists, also showed the sadness that affected modern people, especially women whose opportunities were limited by strict social rules.

The Impressionists were also revolutionary in the ways that they painted. During the Renaissance, painters had adopted a certain viewpoint, or **perspective,** in their work. They established rigid scientific rules of perspective that were accepted for centuries. There were also fixed ideas about picture composition—how the subject should be positioned in the picture—and framing, meaning what the frame, or edge of the picture, could cut off.

The Impressionists began to develop their own theories of perspective, color, and composition. From the mid-1800s new ideas arrived in France from abroad. A universal exhibition, held in Paris in 1855, exposed artists to art from non-European cultures. They realized that the rules they had been taught were not shared by other cultures. The Impressionists found the paintings and prints from Japan particularly influential. More art from Japan was available at a second exhibition in 1867.

The Impressionists loved Japanese art. Degas adopted Japanese-style viewpoints and styles of framing. Manet used Japanese-style coloring that simplified and flattened skin tones and reduced shadows. Monet began to eliminate detail to enhance the effect of the picture as a whole. Gustave Caillebotte shortened the perspective of his paintings and used unusual viewpoints similar to the ones he saw in Japanese prints.

Street in Paris, A Rainy Day, by Gustave Caillebotte (1877)
During the 1800's Paris was reborn as a modern city. Streets were widened, and boulevards and parks were created. Cafés, concert halls, and large public buildings were opened. Life in this new city fascinated many Impressionists. Caillebotte painted the extraordinary changes he saw in the city at this time.

The art establishment had rules for color as well. Artists were taught to paint on a dark base, and to paint shadows as black or dark brown. The Impressionists realized that the colors near shadows added color to them, so they were rarely just black or brown. Monet and Manet began to prime their canvases with a white base, which brightened the colors painted over them. Renoir and Pissarro used a bright **palette.** Pissarro claimed to use only the primary colors—red, yellow, and blue—mixing them to make colors such as orange, green, and purple.

Artists were expected to paint in a studio and work in stages: preparatory sketches, detailed studies, and finally the finished piece. Monet, Bazille, Renoir, and Sisley recognized the value of painting outside—**en plein air**—where colors were more vivid. These artists said it was impossible to reproduce the colors and shadows seen in nature by working with sketches back in the studio. Newly developed paint tubes meant they could more easily use oil-based paints outdoors.

The development of the camera also helped the Impressionists. It captured a moment in time and showed details of human and animal movement that had previously not been revealed. Photographs were also used as the starting point of many Impressionist works. For example, Monet's *Women in the Garden* was based on photographs from Bazille's family album.

Impressionism also owes much to events that occurred in 1863. That year, the **Salon** rejected work by hundreds of artists, including a painting by Manet called *Luncheon on the Grass.* Many artists complained to Emperor Napoleon III, and he ordered another exhibition to be held that would include works refused by the Salon. This was called the **Salon des Refusés.** Although Manet's painting grabbed the headlines, Pissarro and Cézanne also had work exhibited. The Salon des Refusés was important because it strengthened the commitment of radical artists and undermined the prestige of the official Salon. It also identified Manet as the head of the radical new art movement.

Impressionists met to discuss ideas in many cafés, but the most important one was the Café Guerbois on Rue des Batignolles, in Paris. Manet frequented the café, and artists with studios nearby, such as Bazille, Caillebotte, Cézanne, Degas, Monet, Pissarro, and Renoir, often came to meet him there. The Café Guerbois also attracted writers who promoted the new art, including Émile Zola, Stéphane Mallarmé, and Charles Baudelaire. Art critics called the painters who visited the Café Guerbois "*L'École des Batignolles,*" or the Batignolles

School. Several artists said they disliked the heated discussions about art, but all admitted they had learned from them.

The **Franco-Prussian War** of 1870–1871 between France and Prussia ended in defeat for France. An uprising by Parisian Republicans and workers who were unhappy with the new government, The Third Republic, followed the war. Known as the **Paris Commune,** the uprising was controlled with great brutality in May 1871. The war affected many artists. Monet and Pissarro left for Great Britain, and several artists served in the military. Bazille was killed. War and political rebellion created an atmosphere that was unfriendly toward artistic revolutionaries. The public remained suspicious of the Impressionists for many years.

A Girl with a Basket of Fruit, by Frederick Leighton (c.1862–1863) *Imaginary figures based on ancient Greek and Roman myths were popular subjects for traditional artists whose work was accepted at the Salon.*

Several female artists joined the Impressionists. Social customs were against women becoming artists. No state education in Fine Arts was available for women. The Écoles des Beaux-Arts did not admit women until 1897. Women also faced domestic pressure to marry and have families. The Impressionists recognized female artists for their abilities. Women occupied important organizational positions within the Impressionist group.

The Impressionist exhibitions

Deciding not to submit work to the Salon, the Impressionists held their own series of eight exhibitions. The first one opened on April 15, 1874. The art critic Louis Leroy wrote a critical review called "The Exhibition of the Impressionists." Leroy created the word *Impressionist* to describe the art in the exhibition, such as Monet's *Impression: Sunrise*. His review gave the new style a name. The third exhibition, held in 1877, was the first to be called an Impressionist exhibition by the artists themselves.

The Impressionist period was very short—a little more than 20 years. But it changed art forever. All art that has followed it has either developed from or has been a reaction to Impressionism.

Impression: Sunrise, by Claude Monet (1873)
It is believed that Monet took less than an hour to paint this picture, which gave a name to the Impressionist revolution.

Jean-Frédéric Bazille (1841–1870)

- Born on December 6, 1841 in Montpellier, France
- Died November 28, 1870 in Beaune-la-Rolande, France

Key works

The Artist's Family on a Terrace near Montpellier, 1867–1868
View of the Village, 1868
Studio in the Rue de la Condamine, 1870

Frédéric Bazille's tall figure dominates several paintings by fellow Impressionists. The writer Émile Zola described him as "blond, tall, and slim, very distinguished," and said he had "all the noble qualities of youth: belief, loyalty, delicacy." Camille Pissarro called him "one of the most gifted among us."

▮▮ *The Artist's Family on a Terrace Near Montpellier*, by Frédéric Bazille (1867–1868)
*In 1867 the **Salon** rejected Bazille's first version of this painting. Bazille reworked it, and his second version was accepted in 1868. Émile Zola praised Bazille's contemporary subject matter and "love of truth." Bazille painted himself on the far left side of the picture.*

Jean-Frédéric Bazille was born into a wealthy, Protestant, wine-making family. He had several sisters. Art collector Alfred Bruyas, a family friend, stimulated the young man's interest in art. Bazille's family, however, wanted him to be a doctor. He began medical school in Montpellier in 1859, but he lacked interest and grew unhappy. In 1862, a compromise was reached. Bazille's family allowed him to study both medicine and art in Paris. He enrolled at the **atelier** of Charles Gleyre.

Bazille was an enthusiastic art student. He met other students—Alfred Sisley, Claude Monet, and Pierre-Auguste Renoir—who shared his convictions. They began to paint outdoors, or **en plein air.** Artists— even those who did preparatory sketches outside —were taught to complete their work in a studio. Bazille and his friends believed a painting should reflect reality, which could only be achieved if it was completed outside. They were criticized by the **art establishment.** In May 1863, Bazille and Monet went to the Fontainebleau Forest outside Paris. Bazille wrote, "I have been with my friend Monet, who is quite good at landscapes; he has given me advice. The forest is truly wonderful."

Art took up Bazille's time, and his medical studies suffered. In 1864, after a painting trip to Honfleur, Normandy, with Monet, Bazille learned he had failed his medical exams. Supported by his parents, he decided to pursue a career in art. A generous allowance enabled him to help friends. For example, in 1865, he invited Monet to share his studio. In 1866, Bazille submitted two canvases to the **Salon.** One was *Girl at a Piano.* "I chose [a subject from] the modern period . . . and that is what will get me rejected," he said. Sure enough, Bazille's painting was rejected. However, his second submission, a still life, was accepted.

In January 1867, Bazille and Renoir rented a studio on the Rue Visconti. Monet joined them in September. That year, the Salon rejected Monet's *Women in the Garden.* Bazille bought it for 2,500 francs, paying 50 francs a month.

In 1868, Bazille and Renoir rented a studio closer to the Café Guerbois, a meeting place for radical artists. In 1869, the Salon accepted *View of the Village,* one of Bazille's best paintings. In 1870, *Summer Scene, Bathers* was shown. Success seemed to beckon: "I am delighted. . . . Everyone . . . talks about it." Then in July, France declared war on Prussia. Bazille wanted to help his country. He joined the *Zouaves,* a military group with bright uniforms.

In November 1870, during a skirmish at Beaune-la-Rolande, France, a Prussian sniper shot and killed Bazille.

Gustave Caillebotte (1848–1894)

- Born August 19, 1848 in Paris, France
- Died February 21, 1894 in Petit-Gennevilliers, France

Key works

The Floor Scrapers, 1875
Pont de l'Europe, 1876
Street in Paris, A Rainy Day, 1877
Self-Portrait, 1892

For years, Gustave Caillebotte was the least famous Impressionist artist. His work was not well-known until museums started collecting it in the 1960s. Born in Paris in 1848, Caillebotte grew up in Petit-Gennevilliers, outside Paris. His father made a fortune by supplying bedding to the French army. When he died in 1873, he left Caillebotte and his brothers, Martial and René, very wealthy. Caillebotte enrolled at the École des Beaux-Arts that same year.

Caillebotte had many interests. He studied engineering and boat-building before he took up art. He enjoyed rowing, raced yachts, and was an enthusiastic gardener.

The Floor Scrapers, by Gustave Caillebotte (1875)
Caillebotte's best-known works are superbly executed scenes of city life. He was one of the few painters to portray working men.

Caillebotte's boating knowledge brought him into contact with Claude Monet when Caillebotte helped him build a boat studio. Pierre-Auguste Renoir also shared Caillebotte's interest in boats. They often sailed on the River Seine together. Renoir later immortalized Caillebotte in *The Luncheon of the Boating Party*. Caillebotte also got Monet interested in gardening. Gardens later became Monet's favorite **motif.**

Caillebotte showed several paintings at the second Impressionist exhibition in 1876. He continued to contribute to Impressionist exhibitions until 1882. He also helped organize them, using his diplomatic skills to soothe disagreements. Caillebotte's paintings recorded the rise of social groups that owed their existence to the development of the modern city. He was especially interested in the urban middle class. Caillebotte often used unusual viewpoints and was fascinated by dramatic **perspective.**

By the mid-1880s Caillebotte was less involved with the exhibitions. One reason was the arguments that split the Impressionist movement into factions. His painting style developed beyond Impressionism. He inspired several **Neo-Impressionist** artists.

However, he remained friends with several Impressionists, and supported them financially by paying high prices for their paintings. He gave money to buy Édouard Manet's *Olympia* for the French nation in 1889. He also attended monthly Impressionist dinners between 1890 and 1894, where he and Renoir would argue ferociously. Renoir delighted in teasing Caillebotte, whose face turned red with anger. Despite these quarrels, the two remained firm friends.

Caillebotte remained a bachelor all his life. He and his brother, Martial, were close, and shared a house in Petit-Gennevilliers until Martial got married in 1887. Caillebotte also shared this house with Charlotte Berthier. She is often described as his housekeeper. Little is known about her, except that she and Caillebotte were devoted companions. He left her the house and an income in his will.

Toward the end of his short life, Caillebotte stopped collecting pictures and exhibiting. He died on February 21, 1894, at age 45, of what was described as "pulmonary congestion"—probably tuberculosis.

■■ *Self-Portrait*, by Gustave Caillebotte (1892)
This self-portrait was painted two years before Caillebotte died.

Mary Cassatt (1844–1926)

- Born May 22, 1844, in Allegheny City (now part of Pittsburgh) Pennsylvania
- Died June 19, 1926 near Paris, France

Key works
Little Girl in a Blue Armchair, 1878
Woman and Child Driving, 1879
Mother About to Wash Her Sleepy Child, 1880

Born in 1844, Mary Cassatt was the daughter of a wealthy banker, Robert Cassatt. Her mother, Katherine, was well-educated and spoke French fluently. Cassatt was very close to her sister, Lydia. Cassatt is considered an Impressionist because of her interest in the everyday lives of modern women.

Mary Cassatt, Seated with Photographs, by Edgar Degas (1884) *Edgar Degas included Cassatt in several of his paintings. He was a good friend, and had a major influence on her work.*

Cassatt's interest in art was stimulated during a five-year family visit to Europe, between 1850 and 1855. As a teenager she studied art privately, and between 1861 and 1865 she attended the Pennsylvania Academy of the Fine Arts. Although he had supported her while she studied, her father opposed her desire to be an artist, thinking it was not a suitable career for a woman. However, Cassatt was strong-willed and independent-minded. Her father soon agreed to let her focus on art. Cassatt returned to France in 1866. She enrolled in the **atelier** of Charles Chaplin, who organized women-only art classes. She also copied **Old Masters** in the Louvre. In 1868, she had a painting accepted at the **Salon.**

When the **Franco-Prussian War** broke out in 1870, Cassatt fled back to Pennsylvania. In 1872, she returned to Europe, visiting the museums of Italy, Spain, and Holland before arriving in Paris in 1874. She grew unhappy with the French **art establishment** but remained aloof from the Impressionists. However, the following year she saw work by Edgar Degas. She claimed it changed her life. She continued to submit work to the Salon, but her disenchantment grew when a picture that was rejected in 1875 was accepted after she darkened the background.

In 1877, after the Salon again rejected Cassatt's work, a friend brought Degas to Cassatt's studio. They formed a friendship that was to last a long time. He invited her to join the Impressionists. "I accepted with delight. I could work in complete independence, without . . . the eventual judgment of a jury."

Later in 1877, Cassatt's parents and her sister, Lydia, settled in Paris. Lydia became Cassatt's favorite model. Family life—especially the mother and child theme—became Cassatt's principal artistic **motif.** However, her pictures often emphasized women in domestic settings, to show the lack of opportunities that were open to women. Lydia's death in 1882 upset Cassatt deeply. Cassatt exhibited with the Impressionists in 1879, 1880, and 1881. She also helped organize the 1886 Impressionist exhibition, the final one. Her work attracted excellent reviews.

Cassatt began to experiment with printmaking, making pictures from inked metal printing plates. In 1891, she exhibited Japanese-influenced prints. In 1893, Cassatt was invited to create a mural for the Women's Building at the World's Columbian Exposition in Chicago. The title of her mural was *Modern Woman.*

Cassatt's father died in 1891, and her mother died four years later. Her inheritance enabled her to buy the Château de Beaufresne, near Paris. In 1898, she visited the United States for the first time in 20 years. Around this time, Cassatt's eyesight grew worse. An operation to remove **cataracts** in 1911 was unsuccessful. By 1914, she had stopped painting. Instead she helped her friend, Louisine Havermayer, and Louisine's husband, H. O. Havermayer, build their famous art collection.

Mary Cassatt died at Beaufresne on June 19, 1926. Though she often painted mothers and children, she never married, and she had no children of her own.

■■■ *Woman and Child Driving,* by Mary Cassatt (1879)
In this painting, Lydia Cassatt drives a carriage with Odile Fèvre, Degas's niece, at her side. The woman looks nervous, while the child is lost in thought.

Paul Cézanne (1839–1906)

- Born January 19, 1839 in Aix-en-Provence, France
- Died October 22, 1906 in Aix-en-Provence, France

Key works

Dr. Gachet's House at Auvers, 1873
Portrait of Victor Chocquet, 1875–1877
Still Life with Compotier, 1879–1880

Though he is best known as a **Post-Impressionist,** Paul Cézanne made an important contribution to Impressionism during a short period of his career. He was the eldest child of Louis-Auguste Cézanne, a successful banker. He had two sisters, Marie and Rose. His mother, Elizabeth Aubert, was a full-time housewife, similar to most middle-class women of the time. Cézanne was a gentle but temperamental child. A good student at school, he excelled in math, Latin, and Greek. His earliest interests were writing and poetry. One of his school friends was the young Émile Zola. Cézanne often went on long walks with Zola in the countryside. He began to record these in drawings.

▌ Cézanne influenced many Impressionist artists, and was a huge influence on later painters, such as Pablo Picasso and Paul Klee.

When he completed his high school **baccalaureate,** Cézanne obeyed his father and entered the family business. Cézanne studied law for three years, but he painted in his spare time, copying **Old Masters** in Aix Museum. He tried to persuade his father to let him study art. In April 1861, after seeing some paintings Cézanne had done to decorate the family home, his father agreed.

Cézanne left for Paris but found the art world there was hostile to new ideas and forever looking backward. He was intimidated by the snobbery of his fellow students. Depressed, he stopped painting and returned home in the autumn. He took a job in his father's bank but began painting again the following year. He returned to Paris in 1862 and enrolled at the Académie Suisse. It was here that he met Camille Pissarro. Other students made fun of Cézanne's old-fashioned manners and provincial accent, but Pissarro overlooked these. He recognized and encouraged Cézanne's talent.

Cézanne frequented the Café Guerbois and met several artists who became leading Impressionists, including Édouard Manet and Pierre-Auguste Renoir. He was infamous for his scruffy appearance. Throughout the 1860s, Cézanne spent his winters in Paris and his summers in Aix-en-Provence, painting all the time.

In 1870, Cézanne submitted two paintings to the **Salon.** He had done so before without success, and again his work was rejected. This time, however, he was ridiculed as an ignorant rustic in a newspaper. He responded that he would not compromise or produce pictures to please a Salon jury, and declared he would continue to paint things as he saw them.

Later in 1870, he went to L'Estaque, near Marseilles, to escape military service in the **Franco-Prussian War.** He took his model, Hortense Fiquet, with him. The pair returned to Paris in late 1871, and in January 1872 they had a son, also named Paul. The family settled in nearby Auvers, and Pissarro began to direct Cézanne's powerful talent toward landscapes. Cézanne claimed Pissarro was like a father to him.

Cézanne exhibited with the Impressionists in 1874 and 1877, but critics said they could not understand his art. By the late 1870s, Cézanne was frustrated with his lack of recognition compared to Renoir, Pissarro, and Claude Monet.

In April 1886, shortly before his father's death, Cézanne married Hortense. He alternated between Paris and Aix, where he helped care for his elderly mother. In 1895, an art dealer named Ambroise Vollard exhibited Cézanne's work. The exhibition was a success, and Cézanne's reputation was established.

In 1906, Cézanne was caught in a rainstorm while painting. He collapsed by the road. He was later diagnosed with pneumonia. He insisted on going out to paint. His condition worsened, and he died on October 22, 1906.

▮▮▮ *Dr. Gachet's House at Auvers,* by Paul Cézanne (1873)
This painting shows how Cézanne was influenced by Pissarro.
Pissarro said, "If . . . he stays ... at Auvers, he will astonish a lot of
critics who were in too great haste to condemn him."

Edgar Degas (1834–1917)

- Born July 19, 1834 in Paris, France
- Died September 27, 1917 in Paris, France

Key works

Head of a Young Woman, 1867
The Cotton Exchange in New Orleans, 1873
Ballet Rehearsal, 1873–1874
L'Absinthe, 1875–1876
Miss La La at the Cirque Fernando, 1879

Edgar Degas was the son of a Parisian banker named Auguste de Gas. Auguste had been born in Italy. He owned a bank with branches in Paris and Naples, Italy. Degas's mother was an American who was born in New Orleans, Louisiana. Degas's father, an art collector, stimulated his son's interest in painting from the time he was very young. Degas also saw paintings owned by family friends and was especially impressed by Jean-Auguste-Dominique Ingres, the French artist. He began to draw members of his family. His parents encouraged his son to develop his artistic talents as a hobby.

From age eleven, Degas attended France's most prestigious boarding school—the Lycée Louis le Grand in Paris. It was a strict, austere school that prided itself on not teaching any arts subjects. In 1847, Degas's mother died after the birth of her seventh child. Edgar was thirteen when his mother died. Her death had an enormous impact on him. He completed his **baccalaureate** in 1853 and, to comply with his father's wishes, studied law. He left his law studies after less than a year, however, determined to become an artist. After a family argument, he abandoned home and moved to a small apartment. Impressed, his father agreed to let Degas study art. Recognizing the strength of his son's determination and talent, he encouraged and supported him.

In 1853, Degas enrolled at the **atelier** of Louis Lamothe, a former student of Ingres. The year he spent there increased his respect for Ingres. Degas met him only once and was advised, "Draw lines, young man, a great many lines." Degas also enrolled at the École des Beaux-Arts that same year.

Degas was largely self-taught, however. He spent many months copying in the Louvre and would return many times in the years to come. He abandoned formal studies in 1856, and traveled to Italy for three years. Taking advantage of his relatives' hospitality, he visited museums in Naples, Rome, and Florence, copying great works, drawing relatives, and discussing art with artists.

Degas returned to Paris in 1859, and moved into a studio on Rue Madame to continue his self-education. His main interests at that time were portraits and **classically** themed paintings, but in 1862, he met Édouard Manet in the Louvre. It was the beginning of a love-hate relationship. Manet persuaded Degas to use the modern world and the people around him as subjects.

The **Salon** juries accepted Degas's work in 1865. In 1869, Degas's painting *Portrait of Mme G.* was accepted. Berthe Morisot described it as "a very pretty painting of a very ugly woman." Despite his success, Degas became frustrated with the Salon juries' ideas of "good" art.

During the **Franco-Prussian War,** Degas joined the National Guard, serving in Paris during the Prussian siege of 1871. He left after the city surrendered. In October 1872, Degas visited New Orleans. He enjoyed America but missed France. "Everything is beautiful [here] but one Paris laundry girl with bare arms is worth it all for such a confirmed Parisian as I am," he wrote to a friend.

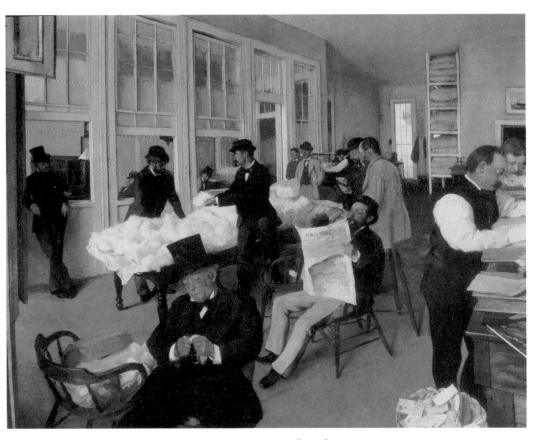

The Cotton Exchange in New Orleans, by Edgar Degas (1873)
This painting shows qualities Degas learned from Manet combined with his own unique style. It is similar to a modern art photograph, producing social realism and a careful and sophisticated picture composition.

19

Degas had a proud, sarcastic, and argumentative manner. But despite this, his reputation grew. The writer Edmond de Goncourt described him as "a bizarre painter—a strange fellow, neurotic, sickly, with bad eyesight—he's always frightened of going blind." But he recognized that Degas was a great painter of the modern world: ". . . the most likely person I've met who can catch the spirit of modern life." Degas visited music halls, concerts, and circuses and attended the ballet three times a week. The performers' disciplined routines and elaborate costumes fascinated him. "You need natural life," he told contemporaries. "I, artificial life." Half of Degas's artwork would be on ballet themes.

Degas submitted nothing to the **Salon** exhibitions after 1870, and he criticized artists who still presented works to them. He helped organize the 1874 Impressionist exhibition as an independent alternative to the Salon.

Degas's father died on a business trip to Naples in 1873. In June 1876, soon after the second Impressionist exhibition, Degas traveled to Naples to discuss the family's financial situation. It was not good. His brother, René, ran the bank so badly that it had incurred huge debts. In August, the intensely proud Degas assumed responsibility for these debts and sold his art collection to avoid

▮▮▮ *The Dance Foyer at the Opera on the Rue le Peletier*, by Edgar Degas (1872)
The world of ballet fascinated Degas, and he completed many pictures, paintings, and sculptures on the subject. By the end of his life, one half of his total works would have ballet as a subject.

bankruptcy. Until now, Degas had not liked to part with his paintings, never believing they were finished, and he sometimes borrowed paintings back to work on them. It was rumored that collectors chained his pictures to their walls to stop him. However, his financial situation now made it important to sell work—much to his regret. By January 1877 Degas had made 20,000 francs, which he paid to the Bank of Antwerp.

At the 1877 Impressionist exhibition, a room was devoted to Degas. Critics praised him. Although the Impressionists wanted to establish themselves as a coherent stylistic force, rivalries increased. Degas tried to keep it from being called the *Exposition des Impressionists*. He described himself as a "realist." He liked to paint under artificial light, having completed many preparatory sketches and watercolors. He disliked painting **en plein air,** once remarking, "The police should shoot down all those easels cluttering up the countryside."

Despite the critics' approval, Degas's finances remained uncertain. Depressed, he wrote to a friend, "To live alone without a family is too hard. . . . Here I am, getting old, and almost penniless. I have organized my life in this world very badly." A mutual friend introduced Degas to Mary Cassatt in 1877. They became close. Some believe Cassatt hoped to marry Degas, but he remained a bachelor all his life.

In 1878, an American friend of Cassatt, Louisine Waldron Elder, lent Degas's *Ballet Rehearsal* to the American Watercolor Society. It was the first Degas exhibited in the United States. It was well-received. The museum of Pau in Southern France bought *The Cotton Exchange in New Orleans*. It became his first work to go to a public collection. Degas's fortunes were improving. That year, Degas read about American photographer Eadweard Muybridge, who used cameras to capture animal and human movement. Degas called photography "magical instantaneity." He bought Muybridge's book, *Animal Locomotion,* and based several pictures of horses on them. Degas later used photographs as the basis of paintings and as artworks in their own right.

At the 1879 Impressionist exhibition, Degas showed 29 works. His influence was more powerfully felt in this exhibition. He insisted that the word *Impressionist* should not be prominent in the exhibition title and was able to include works of many artists who were influenced by him, including Cassatt. Labeled an exhibition by a Group of Independent Artists, it was a commercial success, but critics claimed the Impressionists were finished as a single, unified movement. "You are invited to attend the funeral service . . . of the Impressionists," one wrote.

Degas was a very difficult person to deal with. A journalist called him "aggressive, easily   . . . excited." Paul Gauguin, beginning his own artistic career, witnessed Degas's attempts to force his own way. 'Degas . . . has a perverse spirit that destroys everything." Gustave Caillebotte, who described himself as "a pupil of Degas," grew tired of his stubbornness and bad temper. When Pierre-Auguste Renoir, Alfred Sisley, Paul Cézanne, and Claude Monet did not participate in the 1880 Impressionist exhibition because of Degas, Caillebotte accused him of introducing "disunity into our midst." However, Degas was excluded from the 1882 Impressionist exhibition, and the others returned.

Miss La La at the Cirque Fernando, by Edgar Degas (1879)
Degas visited the Cirque Fernando, a popular Parisian circus, which inspired several works. Miss La La was one of the best-received paintings of the fourth Impressionist exhibition.

Degas could be very kind. When critic Edmond Duranty died, Degas arranged an art sale to help Duranty's companion. He also played matchmaker for Julie Manet, the orphaned daughter of Berthe Morisot.

Degas battled deteriorating eyesight from 1870. He continued to work until five years before his death but bad vision affected his style. Throughout his career he used paints, pastels, and printing techniques. As his eyesight worsened, he abandoned painting and used pastels. By the 1890s, he was also using photography, both to create images and to enable him to continue painting. Similarly, he had often sculpted and modeled during his career. A life-sized wax sculpture, Little Dancer of 14 Years, was shown at the sixth Impressionist exhibition. When his sight became so bad he was unable to use pastels, Degas turned to sculpture.

Degas grew morose. In 1884, at age 50, he wrote, "I always thought I had time; what I didn't do . . . I never gave up hope of starting one fine day. I've hoarded all my plans in a cupboard of which I always carried the key, and I've lost that key." He distanced himself from his contemporaries. He scolded Monet for submitting work to the **Salon** and accepting honors and praise. Gauguin wrote to Camille Pissarro, "Degas has greatly harmed our movement. . . . fortunately art has not suffered from this. . . . Degas is going to end his days more unhappy than the others."

■ *During World War I, as battles raged close to the city, Degas blindly wandered the streets of Paris. He had stubbornly refused to leave his beloved city when it was threatened in 1914.*

In 1886, Degas organized the eighth, and last, Impressionist exhibition. Few original Impressionists participated. Degas shocked many with a series of nude women bathing. Meanwhile, the art dealer Paul Durand-Ruel organized an Impressionist exhibition in New York. It contained 23 works by Degas, which were praised for their "knowledge of life."

Degas encouraged new artists, including Gauguin, Georges Seurat, and Paul Signac, but he grew increasingly isolated. He no longer attended Impressionist dinners and lived a hermit's existence in Paris. His life was littered with ruined friendships. He said, "I quarreled with all the world and with myself." During the **Dreyfus Affair** of the 1890s, Degas became **anti-Semitic.** Pissarro, who was Jewish, had stuck by Degas until now, but this was the final straw. Their friendship crumbled. In 1898, Degas returned to St. Valéry-sur-Somme, where his parents had taken him as a child. Almost blind, he completed what would be his last landscapes.

Financially, Degas was very successful. His art collection included work by Berthe Morisot, Pissarro, Cassatt, Gauguin, Édouard Manet, Vincent van Gogh, and others. But at the end of his life, he was isolated, unable to paint, and surrounded by a collection of masterpieces he could not see to enjoy. He died of a stroke at his Paris home on September 27, 1917. Renoir said, "It is indeed the best for him. . . . Every imaginable kind of death would be better than to live as he was living."

Childe Hassam (1859–1935)

- Born October 17, 1859 in Dorchester, Massachusetts
- Died August 27, 1935 in East Hampton, New York

Key works
Rainy Day, Columbus Avenue, Boston, 1885
Manhattan's Misty Sunset, 1911
Fifth Avenue, April Morning 1917, 1917
Church at Gloucester, 1918

Frederick Childe Hassam was born in Dorchester, Massachusetts in 1859. As a young man he began to use his middle name, Childe, which was the name of a favorite uncle, and sign his name F. Childe Hassam. His family ran a successful hardware business in nearby Boston. However, the business was destroyed in a large fire in 1872, and the family started to fail financially. To help his family, Hassam took a job in the accounting department of the Boston publisher Little, Brown and Company.

In later years, Hassam's ideas about art became more conservative. In February 1913, he criticized the European art on display at the International Exhibition of Modern Art in New York.

Hassam had shown an interest and a talent for art from an early age. His supervisor at work persuaded him to learn the craft of wood engraving. After his apprenticeship, he became a freelance book and magazine illustrator. This enabled him to support himself while he studied art in evening classes at the Boston Art Club. He then studied at the Howell Institute before returning to the Boston Art Club in 1882. He began painting in and around Boston and, during a trip to nearby Gloucester, sold many watercolors. Encouraged, he committed himself to painting.

In 1883, Hassam made his first trip to Europe, stopping first in England, where he was impressed with the work of English painter Joseph Turner. He went on to France and Italy. When he returned, 67 watercolors from his trip were exhibited in Boston. Sales went well and in late 1883, he married Kathleen Maude Doane, whom he had dated for some time.

Many American artists traveled to Paris in the 1880s. American writer Henry James commented, "When today we look for 'American Art' we find it mainly in Paris. When we find it out of Paris, we at least find a good deal of Paris in it." Hassam was no exception. He and his wife visited France in 1886. He was attracted to Impressionism and learned from it, making many rural and urban **plein air** paintings. He also wanted to refine his technique as a painter, so he studied at the Académie Julien in Paris. Like Edgar Degas, he was a strong believer in **draftsmanship** and the importance of line.

The Hassams returned to the United States in 1889 and settled in New York City. Impressionism had become popular, and Hassam's style put him in the center of an emerging group of American Impressionists. He completed many landscapes of rural New England but is best-known for his cityscapes of New York City.

In 1898, Hassam was one of several artists who claimed to be unhappy with the way the American National Academy of Design displayed paintings at their annual show and resigned to form their own group—The Ten. In fact, their resignation was a ploy to draw public attention to their exhibitions. The Ten exhibited together for the next twenty years.

During World War I, Hassam produced many popular patriotic paintings, often featuring American flags. *Fifth Avenue, April Morning 1917* was seen as the ultimate development of his Impressionist style. In later years, Hassam rediscovered his interest in printmaking: "I began my career in the graphic arts, and I am ending it in the graphic arts." After a long illness, he died at home in East Hampton, New York on August 27, 1935.

Manhattan's Misty Sunset, by Childe Hassam (1911)
Hassam is famous for cityscapes of New York. In this painting he used the skyline that visitors were calling "the eighth wonder of the world" as a subject.

Édouard Manet (1832–1883)

- Born January 23, 1832 in Paris, France
- Died April 30, 1883 in Paris, France

Key works

The Spanish Guitar Player, 1861
Luncheon on the Grass, 1863
Olympia, 1863
The Execution of Emperor Maximilian, 1868–1869
A Good Glass of Beer, 1873
Bar at the Folies-Bergère, 1881–1882

Édouard Manet was the son of a wealthy judge, Auguste Manet. His mother was Eugénie-Desirée. He attended the school of Abbé Poilup in Vaurigard and boarded at the Collège Rollin from the age of twelve. His father hoped he would study law, but Manet was not a good student. He even had to stay at school for an extra year. However, he had a talent for drawing, and at age sixteen announced he wanted to be an artist. Horrified, his family promptly enrolled him as a naval cadet. However, his family's resistance crumbled after he made a single voyage to Brazil, during which the boredom of "nothing but sea and sky" was interspersed with seasickness. Manet was asked to retouch the colored rinds of the cargo of cheese they were carrying, and the oil paints he used led to an outbreak of lead poisoning in Brazil. In Rio de Janeiro, he caught **syphilis,** which would eventually kill him.

In 1850, Manet entered the **atelier** of Thomas Couture. He stayed for six years and developed his technique by copying works by the Spanish painters Velásquez and Goya. He also visited museums in the Netherlands, Germany, Austria, and Italy. In the Netherlands in 1851, Manet met Suzanne Leenhoff, a music teacher. They had a son, Léon, in 1852. Manet kept both his wife and son a secret, fearing his father would disapprove of Suzanne and stop his allowance. Manet married Suzanne in 1863, after his father's death.

In 1861, the **Salon** accepted two of Manet's paintings. However, in 1863 they rejected *Luncheon on the Grass*. It then became the centerpiece of the **Salon des Refusés.** To some, Manet's picture of a nude woman sitting between two men in modern dress was a triumph. To others, it was pornography. Arguments also followed the Salon's acceptance of another painting, *Olympia*, in 1865. Manet interpreted **classical** ideas in this painting. He based the subject of *Olympia* on a painting by an **Old Master** painter, Titian. He used Titian's composition, but updated it so the subject resembled a modern woman. The **art establishment** did not accept Manet's decision to present modern life in his paintings.

Many young artists, including Frédéric Bazille, Claude Monet, Edgar Degas, Pierre-Auguste Renoir, Camille Pissarro, and Paul Cézanne, congregated around Manet in the Café Guerbois. He was charismatic, funny, and attractive. In the left-wing newspaper, *L'Evènement*, writer Émile Zola praised Manet as "a man of great sensitivity and kindness." Manet had great influence. At the 1868 Salon, critics said Renoir's *Lise with a Parasol* was a Manet imitation. Many believed Manet had radical views. Some art historians consider him a wealthy revolutionary who wanted to replace the empire with a republic. But Manet enjoyed the privileges of his class and sought official recognition. He wrote, "Monsieur Manet has . . . no intention of overthrowing old methods of painting."

■■ *The Execution of Emperor Maximilian, by Édouard Manet (1868–1869)*
This painting is often cited as evidence of Manet's republicanism. In 1863, France invaded Mexico and made Maximilian, the brother of the Austrian emperor, Emperor of Mexico. When the Mexicans revolted, the French abandoned Maximilian, and he was executed. Manet, like others, blamed Emperor Napoleon III of France for Maximilian's death. To emphasize this point, he painted the firing squad in French uniform.

He never exhibited with the Impressionists and used his portrait skills to flatter influential people. Degas said, "[Manet] felt only one ambition, to become famous and earn money."

In 1869, Manet tackled the problem occupying his friends—how to capture a single moment on a quickly painted canvas. He spent the summer in Boulogne, on the French coast, and completed several works that captured events as they happened. "One does not paint a landscape, a seascape, a figure," he later said. "One paints the impression of an hour of the day."

Manet had a fierce temper. In 1870, he fought a duel with a friend and art critic Edmond Duranty. Duranty was slightly injured, but he and Manet were friends again within hours. Manet and Degas often argued. Degas said Manet never did a brushstroke "without the masters in mind." Manet never let Degas forget it was he who encouraged Degas to portray modern life.

Manet sent his wife and son to the country for the duration of the **Franco-Prussian War.** During the **Siege of Paris,** Manet joined the National Guard. He visited Berthe Morisot's home with his brother, Eugène. Manet enjoyed the war and, Morisot wrote, "spent . . . the siege changing uniform." Manet asked artist Eva Gonzalès to paint him in uniform.

Eva Gonzalès

Eva Gonzalès was born into an aristocratic Monaco family on May 5, 1849. She produced many works—85 were shown at a **retrospective** in 1885. In 1867, she enrolled at the **atelier** of Charles Chaplin in Paris. In 1869, she met Manet, who asked her to model. She agreed to do this in exchange for art lessons, much to her father's disapproval, because he did not think a career in art was appropriate for a woman.

Gonzalès submitted *The Little Soldier* (1870), based on a painting by Manet, to the 1870 **Salon.** She spent the Franco-Prussian War in Dieppe. She stayed inside the official system and continued to submit pieces to the Salon, although they were often rejected. She did not participate in the Impressionist exhibitions. Her models were often drawn from her immediate circle, especially her sister, Jeanne, and husband, Henri Guérard.

In 1883, five days after the birth of her first child, Eva Gonzalès died of an obstruction of a blood vessel. She was 34 years old.

He reported the hardships to Suzanne. In September he wrote, "We eat meat only once a day." In November: "Marie's big cat has been killed, and we suspect somebody in the house; it was for a meal, of course, and Marie was in tears!" Manet left for the Pyrenees after Paris surrendered in January 1871. He returned in time to see the suppression of the **Paris Commune** by the government. He demonstrated his sympathy for the Communards in a series of etchings.

Manet's fortunes improved after the war. He sold work to art dealer Paul Durand-Ruel. His painting, *A Good Glass of Beer,* was praised at the 1873 **Salon.** Believing the **art establishment** was ready to accept him, he did not take part in the 1874 Impressionist exhibition. However, in 1876 two of his submissions to the Salon were rejected. Manet organized shows at his studio. He had 4,000 visitors to these, which confirmed his celebrity status.

In 1877, Manet developed the first symptoms of locomotor ataxia, a crippling illness associated with **syphilis.** In 1881, Manet received a Second-Class Medal from the Salon and was appointed Knight of the Legion of Honor. He complained that this recognition had arrived too late. By 1883, Manet was desperately ill. He developed gangrene in his left leg, and it was amputated on April 19. His fame made his illness a public event. Daily bulletins were posted outside his home. He died at Rueil, near Paris, on April 30, at age 51.

■■■ *Édouard Manet was the most notorious artist of his day. Because his subjects—nudes in modern settings; pictures with republican sympathies; informal portraits—outraged the artistic establishment, he became a hero to younger artists and had a huge impact on Impressionism.*

Claude Monet (1840–1926)

- Born on November 14, 1840 in Paris, France
- Died on December 5, 1926 in Giverny, France

Key works

Camille: Woman in the Green Dress, 1866
The Thames and the Houses of Parliament, 1871
Impression: Sunrise, 1872–1873
Haystacks, 1890–1891
The West Front of Rouen Cathedral, 1892
The Water Lilies, 1916–1926

Claude Monet is the best-known Impressionist. He was born in Paris in 1840. His family moved to Le Havre when he was five. His father was a wholesale grocer and merchant who supplied equipment for boats. His parents and teachers thought young Monet was undisciplined. "It seemed like a prison," he later said of school, "and I could never bear to stay there." Art was his only interest, and he earned a reputation for doing caricatures, or cartoon portraits of teachers. He earned money drawing caricatures of tourists on local beaches.

Monet left school at age fifteen. He was soon earning more than his teachers doing caricatures to order. In 1858, he met a local artist, Eugène Boudin, who recognized the young man's talents and steered him toward painting—especially landscapes and open-air painting. Monet later claimed Boudin "tore the veil from my eyes." Monet and his father had a difficult relationship. Monet maintained that his father wanted to crush his artistic ambitions. In fact, his father encouraged them, believing they would instill discipline into his son. He let Monet study in Paris. In 1859, Monet enrolled at an **atelier** and wasted much of his time.

Monet's father believed he could put a stop to his son's unruly ways. Like most young men of the time, Monet was liable for military service. Wealthy parents often paid a substitute to serve in their son's place, but Monet's father refused to help unless his son abandoned his carefree lifestyle. Monet greeted this with what he called "a superb gesture of indifference," and signed up for seven years in the military.

Monet joined a regiment in French Algeria in 1860. He came home two years later with typhoid. Warned that a return to the army might kill him, Monet's father bought him out. Monet's aunt then offered to sponsor him if he agreed to study art seriously. Monet agreed. In November 1862, he joined the Paris studio of Charles Gleyre. He befriended fellow students Pierre-Auguste Renoir, Alfred Sisley, and Frédéric Bazille. Rebellious by nature and certain of his ideas, Monet became their leader. Although he disliked the idea of being taught, he stayed for eighteen months, until Gleyre's studio went bankrupt. Later, Claude Monet claimed he studied there for only a week and refused to acknowledge Gleyre's teaching. Monet's stubbornness continued to frustrate his family in Le Havre. His allowance was often cut.

In 1863, Monet and Bazille traveled to the Fontainebleau Forest to paint **en plein air.** Monet believed paintings—even portraits—could only be created realistically in natural light. In 1865, Monet made his first submissions to the **Salon**—two seascapes. A critic wrote of one of them, "Monet, unknown yesterday, has . . . made a reputation by this picture alone." In 1866, Monet exhibited *Camille: Woman in the Green Dress* based on his model and companion, Camille Doncieux, whom he met in 1863. Writer Émile Zola praised him, and Monet's family, pleased with the attention, resumed paying his allowance.

▮▮ Claude Monet is shown here in front of his famous series The Water Lilies.
In old age, Monet dedicated himself to completing this last, great series of paintings as a celebration of the glory of France.

Money was a persistent worry for Monet. His allowance was irregular; his expenses—including rent, materials, and food—were considerable; and he was not selling any work. In 1866, Monet fled to Ville-d'Avray, in the Ile de France, to escape creditors—people to whom he owed money. Late that year, Camille became pregnant. In July 1867, Monet revealed her condition to his family, hoping for their sympathy. Monet's father invited him to come home— and leave Camille in Paris. Desperate, Monet went to Le Havre. He could not even raise the train fare to be with Camille when she gave birth to their son, Jean. Monet finally returned to Paris in the autumn to be with Camille and Jean. He joined Bazille and Renoir at their studio.

The year 1868 did not start well. Monet and Camille were so poor they could not buy coal. "My painting doesn't go . . . I see everything black . . . money is always lacking." The family stayed on the Normandy coast. "I spend my time

■■■ *La Grenouillère*, by Claude Monet (1869)
Working without preparatory stages, the paintings quickly produced at La Grenouillère by both Monet and Renoir perfectly captured the sparkle of the water, the light in the trees, and the bright reflections of the tourists' clothes.

out of doors," he wrote to Bazille. "On the pebble beach . . . or I go into the country. . . . And then in the evening, my dear friend, I find a good fire and a cozy little family in my cottage." His submissions to the **Salon** were rejected. Artistically, Monet's breakthrough came in 1869, when he and Renoir painted at La Grenouillère (The Frog Pond), a restaurant on the River Seine.

Monet spent the summer of 1870 painting in Le Havre and the resort of Trouville. In June, he and Camille married. Still a member of the military reserve and likely to be called up, Monet fled to London at the outbreak of the **Franco-Prussian War.** Camille and Jean stayed behind, in the care of Boudin. Monet spent time with Camille Pissarro in London and met art dealer Paul Durand-Ruel, also a refugee, and persuaded him to take his paintings. Monet produced many paintings while in London and often returned in later years. He went back to France after the fall of the **Paris Commune** and settled in Argenteuil with Camille. His fame, if not fortune, was increasing. Friends helped, but his newest patron was a pretentious businessman, Ernest Hoschedé.

In 1873, still frustrated by his lack of recognition, Monet returned to the idea of a group exhibition, which he had discussed with Bazille years before. By 1874, the dream was a reality, and exhibitors were invited to show what they liked. At this first exhibition, Monet's painting *Impression: Sunrise* gave the whole Impressionist movement its name.

In 1876, Monet and Hoschedé's wife, Alice, formed a close relationship. Two years later, Hoschedé lost his fortune. He sold his Impressionist paintings at an auction that made little money. Alice and her six children joined the Monets in their house in Argenteuil. Ernest moved to Paris to pursue what he called "an impoverished bachelor life." Camille gave birth to a second son, Michel, in 1878. She never recovered from the birth, and by 1879 she was very sick.

Marie Bracquemond

Marie Quiveron Bracquemond was born in 1841. She studied under the great French painter Jean-Auguste-Dominique Ingres. In 1869, she married Félix Bracquemond, an etcher and printmaker. He introduced her to the Impressionists. Of Monet she said, "He opens my eyes and makes me see better." Bracquemond exhibited with the Impressionists in 1879, 1880, and 1886.

Félix grew jealous of her talent and did not allow her to show her work to visitors. Pierre, their son, recorded her difficulties. Bracquemond abandoned painting around 1890. She continued to support the Impressionist principles of art until her death in 1916.

Monet pawned their possessions to pay for medical care. He wrote to a friend, "Please . . . retrieve from the pawnshop the locket. . . . It is the only memento that my wife has been able to keep and I should like to tie it around her neck before she leaves forever." Camille died on September 5, 1879. As she lay dying, Monet captured her death on canvas. "I caught myself . . . searching for the . . . colored gradations [changes in color] that death was imposing on her motionless face." Monet later compared his experience of seeing everything in terms of art to the life of an animal harnessed to a millstone.

In 1880, Monet agreed, under pressure from an art dealer, to exhibit at the **Salon**—to the fury of Pissarro and Edgar Degas. He also began to hold one-man shows, encouraged by Durand-Ruel. These were more successful and actually made money. By 1882, Monet was earning a lot of money through Durand-Ruel. Monet contributed to one more Impressionist exhibition, in 1882, and submitted nothing to the Salon after 1880. He had grown so famous that he did not need to exhibit any more.

Monet's domestic situation was also more settled. In 1881, he, Alice ,and their respective children moved to a house at Poissy. They eventually married in 1891, after Hoschedé's death. In 1883, the family moved to Giverny, which remained Monet's home until his death.

Financial security led Monet toward the production of paintings in series— sets of pictures using the same subject that differed according to the time of day, environmental conditions, or season. He began his series paintings in the 1870s, with a sequence of views of Westminster Bridge in London and the steam-enshrouded Gare Saint-Lazare railroad station in Paris. Serialism became one of his most original contributions to art—an attempt to show the passage of time on a single subject. In 1891, he exhibited fifteen canvases of haystacks. He completed sequences of the *Valley of the Creuse* (1889), *Poplar Trees on the Epte River* (1891), *The West Front of Rouen Cathedral* (1892), and *The River Thames* (1899–1903). Julie Manet, the fourteen-year-old daughter of Berthe Morisot, recalled a visit to Giverny in 1893, "Monsieur Monet showed us his 'cathedrals.' There are twenty-six. . . . These pictures . . . are an admirable lesson in painting." Serialism brought its own problems, however. In May 1889, Monet wrote to Alice complaining he had to employ workmen to remove the leaves from an oak tree in order to finish a winter landscape.

Alice died in 1911. Monet, now more than 70, was cared for by one of Alice's daughters, who had married Monet's eldest son, Jean. In 1914, Jean died. Monet was deeply affected by both deaths.

Two events provided the motivation for Monet's great series *The Water Lilies*. In 1912, Monet found out he had **cataracts.** His eyesight deteriorated, and *The Water Lilies* was partly a response to the problems he had distinguishing colors. World War I also gave Monet an incentive. He believed a monumental work would pay tribute to France and establish his reputation. Commissioned by Prime Minister Georges Clemenceau, twelve huge panels recorded the changing reflections on Monet's lily ponds. In 1921, it was decided they would be hung in the Musée de l'Orangerie in Paris. In 1923, an operation on his cataracts allowed Monet to continue working. He worked on *The Water Lilies* until his death on December 5, 1926, at age 86.

The Water Lilies by Claude Monet (1916–1926)
Monet created a water garden at Giverny, and it was here he painted his last, and many believe his greatest, series.

Berthe Morisot (1841–1895)

- Born January 14, 1841 in Bourges, France
- Died March 2, 1895 in Paris, France

Key works
The Mother and Sister of the Artist, 1870
The Cradle, 1872
Young Woman in a Ball Gown, 1876
*Eugène Manet and his Daughter at
   Bourgival,* 1881

Berthe Morisot was the third daughter of Edmé-Tiburce Morisot, the government official in charge of the town of Bourges. The eighteenth-century painter Jean-Honoré Fragonard was a distant relative on her mother's side. Little is known about her childhood, except that she grew up in a supportive environment and liked reading, playing the piano, and modeling clay. The family traveled wherever her father's job took him, but in 1855 they settled in Passy, a suburb of Paris near the wooded Bois de Boulogne. Although she often traveled, Morisot lived in Passy for the rest of her life. Her work often featured the Bois de Boulogne.

Berthe Morisot Holding a Bunch of Violets, by Édouard Manet (1872) *Although the Impressionists were tolerant of women artists, Morisot is sometimes better known as a model than as an artist in her own right.*

In 1857, when Berthe was sixteen, her mother paid for her and her two sisters, Edma and Yves, to take art lessons. Yves lost interest, but Berthe and Edma continued. Because they were women, they were barred from the École des Beaux-Arts, so they took lessons from Joseph-Benoît Guichard. Berthe and Edma decided they wanted to paint **en plein air.** Guichard recommended that they study under the artist Jean-Baptiste Camille Corot, who taught them from 1861 to 1862. Both sisters submitted works to the **Salon** in 1864, and both had paintings accepted. In 1867, Berthe exhibited at a Paris gallery and had two paintings accepted at that year's Salon.

Morisot often copied the **Old Masters** in the Louvre, where she noticed Édouard Manet. Soon after, Manet and Morisot were formally introduced, either by Henri Fantin-Latour or by Edma's fiancé, Adolphe Pontillon. Pontillon had served with Manet during the latter's time as a naval cadet. Morisot was influenced by Manet's technique and emphasis on design.

She encouraged him to experiment with outdoor painting. She also posed for him. Morisot's male colleagues often tried to improve her work. When Manet repainted her picture, *The Mother and Sister of the Artist* , she was furious. Her most common themes were intimate portraits of domestic life. They often featured Edma. By 1874, Morisot had developed her own unique style.

Morisot remained in Paris during the Prussian siege. The hardships and severe food shortages affected her health in later life. Edgar Degas, Manet, and Manet's brother, Eugène, visited her often. Of Degas, Morisot wrote that he was "a little mad, but charmingly witty." She married Eugène Manet in 1874. He tirelessly promoted his wife's talent.

Morisot's interest in outdoor painting and the dramas of everyday life propelled her toward Impressionism. She was the only woman to take part in the 1874 Impressionist exhibition. She showed work at seven of the eight Impressionist exhibitions, only missing the 1879 show after the birth of her daughter. Morisot exerted an influence she would never have enjoyed at the Salon. Her home became a social center for the Impressionists. Her daughter, Julie Manet, became her favorite model. She charted Julie's growth for fifteen years.

By 1880, Morisot was at the height of her powers. Fellow Impressionists admired her work. Eugène Manet died in April 1892. In March 1895, Morisot developed pneumonia. She wrote, "My little Julie, I love you. . . . I shall go on loving you after I am dead; please don't cry for me ..." She died on March 2, 1895, at age 54. After her death, Degas arranged a memorial exhibition. Despite her reputation, Morisot's death certificate records her as without a profession. Her position as an artist was never officially recognized.

The Cradle, by Berthe Morisot (1872)
In this portrait of Edma and her baby daughter, Morisot managed to capture an air of sadness. Edma had been successful at the Salon but found it difficult to paint after her marriage.

Camille Pissarro (1830–1903)

- Born July 10, 1830 in Saint Thomas, Danish West Indies
- Died November 13, 1903 in Paris, France

Key works

Lower Norwood, London: Snow Effect, 1870
Lordship Lane Station, Dulwich, 1871
The Red Roofs: Corner of the Village, Winter Effect, 1877
Portrait of Félix Pissarro, 1881
The Gleaners, 1889
The Rooftops of Old Rouen, Grey Weather, 1896
The Place du Théâtre Français, 1898

Camille Pissarro was born on Saint Thomas, an island in the Caribbean. His father's family originated from Portugal. They were Marranos—Jews forcibly converted to Christianity by the Catholic organization known as the **Inquisition.** The family later converted back to Judaism. Pissarro's father, Frédéric, traveled from Bordeaux, South West France, to Saint Thomas in 1824 to carry out his late uncle's will. He fell in love with his uncle's widow, Rachel, who came from the Dominican Islands. When she got pregnant, they announced their intention to marry. The synagogue refused to acknowledge the wedding, and they were forced to marry outside the synagogue in 1825.

According to the art historian Joachim Pissarro, a great-grandson of Camille Pissarro, Camille and his three siblings were deemed illegitimate and attended an all-black primary school run by a Protestant body—the Moravian Brethren— instead of the white school. In 1833, the synagogue finally recognized his parents' marriage—and therefore the legitimacy of the children—when Camille was three. There may be other reasons why Frédéric sent Camille to the Moravian school—perhaps because his older siblings were already there, or because of Frédéric's anger at the synagogue. In fact, when he died, Frédéric split his money equally between the church and the synagogue.

The Pissarros ran a clothing store in the port of Charlotte Amalie. Many merchant ships called every week, and Saint Thomas became a major trade center between the Americas, Europe, and Africa. As a boy, Camille spoke French at home, and spoke English and Spanish with the black population of the island. He began to draw, often portraying the black people he saw around him, of whom many were still slaves. He would often revisit the theme of people at work when he became an artist.

Anxious that his son should have a good—that is, French—education, Frédéric sent Pissarro to boarding school in France in 1842. His teachers, recognizing the child's artistic ability, encouraged him to sketch whatever he saw. Pissarro returned to Saint Thomas in 1847 to join the family business. But instead of supervising cargoes, he sketched the vibrant harbor life, frustrating his father. In 1852, unable to persuade his father to let him study art, Pissarro ran off to Venezuela with a Danish artist, Fritz Melbye. "Living in Saint Thomas . . . I could not endure the situation any longer. . . . I abandoned all I had there and fled." He worked in Caracas as an artist for two years.

Finally agreeing to let his son pursue a career in art, Frédéric insisted he should study in Paris. Pissarro returned to the French capital in 1855. He met Armand Guillaumin and Paul Cézanne at the Académie Suisse. He also found like-minded artists at the Café Guerbois. According to art historian John Rewald, Pissarro became "a welcome guest . . . for there was no one . . . who did not feel a deep esteem for this gentle and calm man . . . the most distrustful, most undependable members of the group, Cézanne and [Edgar] Degas, felt real friendship for him."

Soon after he arrived in Paris, Pissarro's parents left their business with a caretaker manager and settled in the French capital. They hired a maid from Burgundy named Julie Vellay. In 1860, Pissarro and Julie began a relationship. Their first child, Lucien, was born in 1863. Although they married in London in 1871, Vellay's low social origins kept her from participating in Pissarro's social life.

When Pissarro's father died in 1865, Pissarro's allowance ended. He was forced to do odd jobs, including painting decorative window blinds with Guillaumin. In 1869, Pissarro and his family moved to Louveciennes. The following year, they fled to London before the Prussian advance, leaving almost all of Pissarro's work behind. Prussian troops stayed in his house and used the artworks as floor coverings. Of 1,500 works, only 50 survived.

▮▮ *Throughout his life, Pissarro was interested in the daily lives of working people and was the most politically active of the Impressionists. Some say this is because of his childhood in the Danish West Indies, where he witnessed the effects of slavery firsthand.*

The Pissarros returned to Paris in June 1871. Camille became an energetic member of the Impressionists and the only one to participate in all of their exhibitions. In 1872, the Pissarros moved to Pontoise. Financial problems continued, and in late 1874 the family had to live with a friend. In 1878, Pissarro wrote, "I am going through a frightful crisis." He owed money, and Julie was pregnant with their fourth child.

Pissarro always nurtured new talent. Many turned to "Père (Father) Pissarro" for advice. He was an inspiring teacher. He never pressed his beliefs. "Scorn my judgment. I cannot hide my opinions from you. Accept only those that accord with your sentiments." He also had a warning: "After 30 years of painting . . . I am [still without money]. Let the younger generation remember!"

■ *The Gleaners,* by Camille Pissarro (1889)
Pissarro tackled many subjects, including landscapes, cityscapes, river scenes, gardens, winter scenes, and images of workers. The Gleaners was painted in Éragny-sur-Epte, where the Pissarro family settled in 1884.

Pissarro was an adventurous artist. During the 1880s he adopted **Pointillism.** At the 1886 Impressionist exhibition, the final one, his work was displayed next to that of the **Neo-Impressionist** artists. He abandoned Neo-Impressionism during the 1890s and re-adopted Impressionism. Some accused him of copying others, but the artist Gauguin retorted in 1895, "He looked at everybody, you say! Why not? Everyone looked at him, too, but denied him. He was one of my masters and I do not deny him!"

Pissarro's reputation grew more slowly than that of his contemporaries, and his family often lived in near poverty. Only his commitment to his art kept his morale high. He was intensely proud of his family. "Such is this family," he wrote, "where art is in the home, where each one of them, young and old, cultivates the rarest flowers of beauty." Sadly in 1897, as Pissarro was finally recognized as a great artist, his eldest son, Lucien (who had also become an artist), had a stroke. In November that year, his third son, Félix, died of tuberculosis. He was only 23.

That same year was also when the **Dreyfus Affair** divided France. Although Pissarro admired Degas, he found his **anti-Semitism** intolerable and ended their friendship. Pissarro suffered eye trouble and underwent several operations. Nevertheless, he painted until the end of his life. Years before he had written, "What I am suffering now is terrible. . . . Yet I think that if I had to start all over again, I would not hesitate to follow the same path." Camille Pissarro died in Paris on November 13, 1903. He was 73 years old.

Armand Guillaumin (1841–1927)

Born in Paris on February 16, 1841, Armand Guillaumin lived in Moulins until he was fifteen, when he was sent back to Paris to work for his uncle. His family opposed his interest in art, and he was forced to study at evening classes. He later worked as a laborer for the Paris Municipality, "working like a slave" three nights a week and painting during the daytime. In 1861, he met Cézanne and Pissarro at the Académie Suisse. In 1868, Guillaumin and Pissarro painted window blinds together. Guillaumin later worked as a laborer again. Pissarro wrote, "Guillaumin . . . works on his painting in the daytime and at his ditch-digging in the evening, what courage!"

Although his poverty prevented him from joining the 1876 and 1879 Impressionist exhibitions, Guillaumin contributed to every other Impressionist exhibition. He also encouraged new painters, including Paul Signac and Georges Seurat. In 1891, Guillaumin won a lottery prize of 100,000 francs and devoted himself to art. He died in June 1927, at age 86.

Maurice Brazil Prendergast (1859–192

- Born October 10, 1859 in St. Johns, Newfoundland, Canada
- Died February 1, 1924 in New York City

Key works
Umbrellas in the Rain, 1899
May Day 1903, Central Park, 1903
Neponset Bay, 1914
Salem Park, Massachusetts, 1918

Maurice Brazil Prendergast was born into a poor family in St. Johns, Newfoundland, Canada, in 1859. He had a twin sister, who died at age seventeen, and a younger brother, Charles. Little is known of his early life.

In 1868, the Prendergasts emigrated from Canada to Boston. Maurice entered an American school, where he studied technical drawing. He left school at fourteen and took a job in a dry goods store, selling men's clothing and accessories. He continued to study art at night school. He often visited the Museum of Fine Arts in Boston and, according to his brother, Charles, also sketched the countryside around Boston.

▮▮ *Prendergast was a painter of both townscapes and country scenes, and is best known for pictures of people outdoors, enjoying themselves.*

By 1891, Maurice and Charles—also an artist—had saved enough money to travel to Europe. They crossed the Atlantic on a cattle boat, which was exporting live cattle to Europe. Maurice stayed in France for more than three years, enrolling at the Académie Julien in Paris in 1891. He also studied at the Académie Colarossi.

Prendergast returned to Boston in 1894 and joined Charles in Winchester, Massachusetts. His art focused on people enjoying their leisure time, walking in the park or on the beach. His first gallery showing was at the Boston Art Club in 1895, and his first one-man show was at the Macbeth Gallery, New York, in 1900. He also spent several years traveling in Europe.

Despite the relative popularity of Impressionism in the United States, Prendergast found it difficult to sell paintings. He and Charles were close and, for both artistic and economic reasons, shared studio space. Charles owned a successful picture framing business and supported his brother financially.

Prendergast exhibited widely and frequently. By 1910, he had developed his own Post-Impressionist style. In 1908, he joined The Eight, a group of artists who broke with traditional styles that were popular in America at the time. The Eight wanted to show "real life" by means of quickly executed drawings, sketches, and paintings. They hoped to develop an authentic American school of painting. The Eight exhibited only once. The show was held in 1908, at the Macbeth Gallery in New York City. Prendergast took part in this show, but none of his paintings were sold. The Eight went on to form the nucleus of The Ash Can School, who painted the growing slums, their poverty-stricken residents, and the increasing number of social outcasts in the United States.

In 1923, very sick in a New York City hospital and shortly before his death, Prendergast won a $1,000 prize and bronze medal from the Corcoran Gallery in Washington, D.C. He is reported to have said, "I'm glad they've found out I'm not crazy, anyway." He died in February 1924, at the age of 65.

Neponset Bay, by Maurice Brazil Prendergast (1914)
Prendergast helped organize the famous 1913 Armory Show at which he also exhibited. Respected by his peers and by discerning collectors and dealers, Prendergast was elected president of the Association of American Painters and Sculptors in 1914.

43

Pierre-Auguste Renoir (1841–1919)

- Born February 25, 1841 in Limoges, France
- Died December 3, 1919 in Cagnes-sur-Mer, France

Key works

Lise with a Parasol, 1867
La Grenouillère, 1869
The Ball at Moulin de la Galette, 1876
Mme Charpentier and Her Children, 1878
Luncheon of the Boating Party, 1881
Young Girls at the Piano, 1892

Pierre–Auguste Renoir was born in Limoges, France, the fifth son of a tailor and a dressmaker. The family moved to Paris in 1846, and Renoir was educated at a free Catholic school run by the Christian Brothers. He showed promise as a musician and sang in the parish choir. At age thirteen, having shown early artistic talent, Renoir was apprenticed to a porcelain painting company, Lévy Frères et Compagnie. He decorated pieces with painted designs in their factory near the Louvre Museum in Paris. When he had free time, he visited the Louvre. He also took drawing lessons from a sculptor named Callouette.

Renoir developed a reputation as a painter of porcelain. He began to decorate fans with fashionable scenes that were used by society ladies. He also painted window blinds. He painted religious scenes on translucent material, in imitation of stained-glass windows, for the mobile tent–churches of missionaries. He was able to save a considerable amount of money and, in 1860, enrolled at the Gleyre **atelier.** Here he met Claude Monet, Frédéric Bazille, and Alfred Sisley. Gleyre encouraged Renoir to copy at the Louvre. Renoir also enrolled for evening classes at the École des Beaux-Arts.

Without a wealthy family to support him, Renoir had to submit work to the **Salon** to build his reputation before he could sell canvases. He exhibited at the Salon for the first time in 1864. He later destroyed the painting, called *La Esmerelda.* During the summer, Renoir painted **en plein air** with Bazille, Monet, and Sisley in Fontainebleau Forest. In 1865, the Salon accepted two of his works. However, the 1865 jury was criticized by Salon members for its tolerance toward artists such as Renoir. The realist qualities of Renoir's work did not please them, and a new, conservative jury rejected his submissions in 1866 and 1867. It was a bitter blow.

Renoir continued to live in poverty. He often relied on the generosity of friends, especially Bazille. He regularly visited the Café Guerbois, where he met

Edgar Degas, Édouard Manet, and writer Émile Zola. He continued to submit pieces to the Salon, with increasing success. His painting of Lise Tréhot—*Lise with a Parasol*—was accepted by the Salon and greeted with acclaim by some critics. However, others accused him of emulating Manet.

Pierre-Auguste Renoir, by Jean-Frédéric Bazille (1867)
Poorer and coming from a more humble background than many of his peers, Renoir was much more focused on selling paintings and making his work popular to make a successful living as an artist.

In 1869, Renoir and Claude Monet painted together at La Grenouillère, a popular restaurant outside Paris. The paintings that the two men made at La Grenouillére were a breakthrough in the development of Impressionism.

During the **Franco-Prussian War,** Renoir joined the army. Posted to Bordeaux, he contracted dysentery. He returned to Paris in April 1871. He was deeply attached to this city. It was a place of animation, color, and excitement where he could secure portrait commissions and meet collectors. Renoir showed seven works at the 1874 Impressionist exhibition. He exhibited again in 1876, 1877, and 1882. He continued to submit works to the **Salon,** to the annoyance of Degas, who thought it the worst kind of betrayal of Impressionist ideals. But the Salon was too important to Renoir, who said, "I'm not going to waste my time bearing a grudge against the Salon."

Renoir's greatest success came at the 1879 Salon when a large group portrait, *Mme Charpentier and Her Children*, was accepted. He did not participate in the 1879 Impressionist exhibition, realizing that many more people would see his work at the Salon and that anything he showed with the Impressionists would be ridiculed simply because it was shown with this group of artists. However, he did hold a one-man show at the offices of *La Vie Moderne*—an arts magazine aimed at promoting the Impressionists. By 1879, Renoir was accepting more portrait commissions.

In 1881, Renoir visited Italy. He painted several views of Venice, confessing to the art dealer Paul Durand-Ruel that most were finished in his Paris studio. In March 1882, Durand-Ruel took charge of the seventh Impressionist exhibition, hoping to restore unity to the group. Renoir exhibited 26 pieces, including *Luncheon of the Boating Party*, which were warmly received.

On the way back from Italy, Renoir visited Paul Cézanne in L'Estaque, in the South of France. Impressed by Cézanne's work and influenced by **classical** pieces he had seen in Italy, Renoir told Durand-Ruel he had "reached the end of Impressionism." He began to develop a harder, carefully structured and more classical style of painting. *The Bathers* (1887) typified this change. Camille Pissarro commented, "I do not understand what he is trying to do." However, many liked it. "I think," Renoir wrote to Durand-Ruel, " I have advanced . . . in the public approval." Commercial pressure forced him to change back to his previous style after three years. Durand-Ruel had spent a lot of time persuading buyers to appreciate Renoir's work. He thought these patrons would be reluctant to accept a change, and would not buy paintings in his new style.

There were also changes in Renoir's personal situation. In 1885, Aline Charigot bore him a son, Pierre. Aline had come to Paris to be a seamstress. Renoir met her in 1880 and used her as a model—notably in *Luncheon of the Boating Party*. When she and Renoir married in 1890, five years after Pierre's birth, Renoir's friends found out about their relationship. Aline and Renoir had two more sons, Jean, born in 1894, and Claude, or Coco, born in 1901. During the 1880s and 1890s, the family lived in the grandly named "Château des Brouillards," a ramshackle collection of buildings in a bad neighborhood in Paris.

■■■ *La Grenouillère*, by Auguste Renoir (1869)
Although Renoir and Monet painted the same scene, Renoir placed greater emphasis on the islet and the people on it, indicating the preference he would always show for the human subject.

Despite the fact that Renoir created some of the most memorable images of women, his attitudes toward women were often less complementary. Similarly, his paintings portrayed working people with great dignity, but his opinions about them were old-fashioned. "Education," he once said to Berthe Morisot's daughter Julie Manet, "is the downfall of the working classes."

In 1888, Renoir suffered his first attack of neuralgia, an illness of the nervous system, which temporarily paralyzed his face. Four years later, in 1892, France honored Renoir, buying his *Girls at the Piano* (1892). There was a major **retrospective** at Durand-Ruel's gallery. In 1894, Aline's cousin, Gabrielle Renard, joined the Renoirs to look after their son, Jean. She stayed for twenty years and became Renoir's model. Many of his paintings were now a family record, and Renoir often returned to the theme of mother and child.

Luncheon of the Boating Party, by Auguste Renoir (1881)
In 1881, Renoir completed this painting that would become one of his most famous works. It features, among others, Renoir's future wife, Aline Charigot (on the left, holding a dog) and artist Gustave Caillebotte (sitting on the right).

In 1896, after the death of Morisot, Renoir and his family took care of her daughter, Julie. Renoir began to suffer from rheumatoid arthritis, a crippling disease of the joints. In time it would almost completely disable him, although he never let it keep him from painting. The family spent more time in Cagnes-sur-Mer, in the South of France. In 1900, Renoir was made a *Knight of the Legion of Honor*. He was later promoted to *Officier* and *Commandant*. He was also celebrated enough to have his work faked by unscrupulous artists and dealers. In 1907, Renoir bought land in Cagnes-sur-Mer and had a house built there.

By 1908, Renoir's work was being shown all around the world, including New York and Venice. He remained approachable and enthusiastic. When questioned by an American painter, he said, "I have no rules and no methods; anyone can look at my materials or watch how I paint." Now unable to walk, Renoir was carried to his studio where he painted from a wheelchair with paintbrushes tied to his crippled hands with ribbons.

Renoir became popular in Germany and was a major influence on the **Expressionists.** By 1913, he had exhibited in Munich, Berlin, Dresden, and Stuttgart. To compensate for failing eyesight, he began to experiment with sculpture and, in 1913, employed a 23-year-old sculptor, Richard Guino, as both teacher and assistant. The years of World War I (1914–1918) were hard for Renoir. In October 1914, his sons, Jean and Pierre, were wounded in action. In June 1915, Aline died, at age 56. She suffered a fatal heart attack after visiting Jean in the hospital.

Renoir was now the most celebrated artist in France. When one of his paintings was displayed in the National Gallery in London in 1917, artists and critics sent him a testimonial, "From the moment your picture was hung . . . we had the joy of recognizing that one of our contemporaries had taken . . . his place among the great masters of the European tradition." Renoir survived into the first year of peace. He died of pneumonia at home in Cagnes-sur-Mer, on December 3, 1919. He was 78 years old.

Alfred Sisley (1839–1899)

- Born October 30, 1839 in Paris, France
- Died January 29, 1899 in Moret–sur–Loing, France

Key works
Snow at Louveciennes, 1874
Foggy Morning, Voisins, 1874
Floods at Port-Marly, 1876
Beside the Loing, Saint-Mammes, 1885

Alfred Sisley was born in Paris to wealthy English parents. His father, William, ran a successful import–export business between France and South America dealing in artificial flowers, silks, feathers, and gloves. His mother was Felicia Sell. Alfred enjoyed a privileged, essentially French upbringing with his brother, Henri, and two sisters, Aline and Emily.

In 1857, as an eighteen-year-old, Sisley was sent by his family to study commerce in London. He spent most of his time in

▮▮ *Alfred Sisley*, by Pierre-Auguste Renoir (1864)
After they met at the Gleyre Atelier, Renoir was a strong influence on Sisley. Sisley is known for his landscapes in the Impressionist style.

museums and art galleries. Sisley was influenced by the Pre-Raphaelites—artists working in London who believed that art should be faithful to nature. However, no examples of the work he completed in London exist today.

By the time he returned to Paris in 1862, Sisley knew he wanted to study art. In contrast to many of his peers, Sisley's father encouraged his son's artistic ambitions and, with a generous allowance, Sisley enrolled at the Charles Gleyre **atelier,** where he met Claude Monet, Pierre-Auguste Renoir, and Frédéric Bazille. He also traveled widely and painted extensively in England and Wales.

Sisley's early life was happy and free of worry, thanks to his allowance. Renoir called Sisley "a delightful human being." According to his own statements about his life, Sisley married Marie-Eugénie Lescouezec, a model and florist who came from Toul, in the Lorraine region of France. Little is known about her. Renoir wrote that she had taken up modeling because "her family had been ruined in some financial venture." Legal evidence suggests that the couple never married. They had two children, Pierre, born in 1867, and Jeanne, born in 1869. Sisley and Marie-Eugénie remained devoted to each other for the rest of their lives.

The 1860s were a good time for Sisley. He began to submit work to the **Salon,** and his first acceptance came in 1866. The **Franco-Prussian War** in 1870 was a turning point in Sisley's life. It is thought that he stayed in France during the war but there is evidence that some of his family, and possibly Sisley himself, spent some time in London. As a consequence of the war, the family business collapsed. The shock affected the health of Sisley's father and he died in 1871. Sisley and his young family were now entirely dependent on his art sales. He painted more and more paintings to sell but suffered profound financial hardship. In 1879, he was evicted for not paying his rent. Helped by a wealthy publisher, the Sisleys settled in Moret-sur-Loing in 1880. In the 1880s, Sisley's work was shown to art dealer Paul Durand-Ruel, but even he could not sell it. In 1897, a major **retrospective** of his work was largely ignored.

In old age, Sisley avoided his former comrades. Asked to name his favorite artists, he pointedly ignored the names of his contemporaries. In October 1898, Marie-Eugénie died, having been nursed devotedly through her illness by her husband. Soon after, Alfred realized his own end was near and contacted his old friend, Monet, who rushed to be with him. Sisley died of cancer of the throat in January 1899. He was 60 years old.

Flood at Port-Marly, by Alfred Sisley (1876)
This is one of several paintings Sisley completed showing the effects a flood had on towns and villages in France.

The Next Generation

It is impossible to overestimate the influence of the Impressionists and their importance for the generation of artists who followed them. Camille Pissarro personally advised and inspired a new generation of artists, including Paul Gauguin, Paul Signac, Georges Seurat, Paul Cézanne, and Vincent van Gogh.

Neo-Impressionism and Pointillism

Neo-Impressionism was both a development of Impressionism and a reaction to it. While the Impressionists sought to be realistic, the Neo-Impressionists claimed that their work was more scientific. Neo-Impressionists such as Signac, Seurat, and for a while, Camille Pissarro, applied a scientific understanding of color to Impressionism to create what they termed **Pointillism**—dots of color that achieve an intense brightness when viewed from a distance. They earned the name *Neo-Impressionists* when they showed works at the 1886 Impressionist exhibition.

Georges Seurat

Georges Seurat was born in Paris in 1859. In 1878, he entered the Ecole des Beaux-Arts to study art. He was interested in science, especially in the way the human eye sees color. His reading on science led him to develop the theory of Pointillism.

In 1884, Seurat joined the **Salon des Indépendents.** Although Seurat chose common Impressionist subjects such as popular entertainment, he adopted traditional techniques of preparation and painting. He also departed from Impressionist ideas when, instead of trying to record scenes objectively, he painted to express his own emotional responses to those scenes.

Post-Impressionism

The **Post-Impressionists** were artists who had moved on from or had been directly influenced by Impressionism—in particular Paul Cézanne, Gauguin, and van Gogh. The term *Post-Impressionism* was first used by English art critic Roger Fry to describe art from the period around 1880 to 1905.

Other influences

Pissarro also advised Matisse, who moved from imitating the Impressionists to **Fauvism.** Pissarro encouraged the young artist Francis Picabia who moved from **Cubism** to **Dadaism** and **Surrealism.** Pablo Picasso, who was arguably the most influential artist of the modern age, had long been inspired by the Impressionists, especially Pierre-Auguste Renoir and Edgar Degas.

Vincent van Gogh

Vincent van Gogh was born in 1853. He grew up in the small town of Zundert in the Netherlands. At age sixteen, he was employed at an art gallery run by his uncle. In 1873, he was sent to work in the London branch of the company.

In 1881, van Gogh returned to Holland to paint. He sold nothing and was supported financially by his brother, Theo. In 1885, he left for Paris, where Theo was working. He discovered the work of the Impressionists and met, among others, Pissarro, Gauguin, and Seurat.

Influenced by Impressionism and Japanese art, van Gogh began to express his own responses to what he saw rather than simply reproduce it. He traveled to Arles, in the South of France, in 1888. Between increasingly frequent periods of depression and nervous breakdowns, he produced an incredible number of canvases. He was frequently hospitalized for his depression, and painted even during his stays at the hospital. In 1890, van Gogh committed suicide. He was just 37 years old. He painted over 800 paintings during his short life.

The influence of the Impressionists was enormous. Impressionism paved the way for other artists to work outside of the regulations required by the **art establishment.** Virtually every movement in modern art developed from Impressionism. Impressionist art changed the way both artists and non-artists see the world around them. Today large numbers of people visit Impressionist exhibitions, demonstrating how popular Impressionist art remains.

The Church at Auvers,
by Vincent van Gogh (1890)
In 1886, after Pissarro met Vincent van Gogh for the first time, he warned that van Gogh "would either go mad or leave the Impressionists far behind." Until he met Pissarro, van Gogh's work had been dark and gloomy. After Pissarro explained his own technique and theory of color, van Gogh began to experiment. He soon developed a colorful and dramatic new technique.

Timeline

1830   Camille Pissarro born

1832   Édouard Manet born

1834   Edgar Degas born

1839   Alfred Sisley and Paul Cézanne born

1840   Claude Monet born

1841   Berthe Morisot, Pierre–Auguste Renoir, and Frédéric Bazille born

1844   Mary Cassatt born

1848   Revolution in France begins; Gustave Caillebotte born

1850   Manet enters the **atelier** of Thomas Couture

1859   Childe Hassam and Maurice Brazil Prendergast born; Monet studies at the Académie Suisse, Paris; Pissarro exhibits at the **Salon**; Bazille studies medicine in Montpellier

1860   Renoir starts at the atelier of Charles Gleyre

1861   Manet's *The Spanish Guitar Player* shown at the Salon; Cézanne arrives in Paris

1862   Morisot takes lessons with artist Corot; Monet and Bazille join the atelier of Charles Gleyre

1863   Manet marries Suzanne Leenhoff; the Salon rejects *Luncheon on the Grass*; **Salon des Refusés** is established

1864   Morisot's work accepted by the Salon; Renoir accepted at the Salon

1865   Salon accepts Manet's *Olympia*; Monet shows two seascapes

1866   *Camille: Woman in the Green Dress* by Monet acclaimed at the
        Salon; Alfred Sisley marries Eugénie Lesconezec

1870   **Franco-Prussian War** begins

1871   Pissarro marries Julie Vellay in London before returning to France

1874   First Impressionist exhibition; Morisot marries Eugène
        Manet; Cassatt studies at the atelier of Charles Chaplin

1876   Second Impressionist exhibition

1877   Third Impressionist exhibition

1879   Fourth Impressionist exhibition

1880   Fifth Impressionist exhibition

1881   Sixth Impressionist exhibition; Manet made a *Knight of the
        Legion of Honor*

1882   Seventh Impressionist exhibition

1886   Eighth (and last) Impressionist exhibition

1889   Fund established to buy Manet's *Olympia* for the French nation

1890   Renoir marries Aline Charigot

1900   Renoir is made a *Knight of the Legion of Honor*

1914   World War I begins

Glossary

anti-Semitic   person who hates or acts against people because they are Jewish

art establishment   people who believed in idealization in art, of both people and places; they tended to reject art that did not fall within their strict definitions

atelier   art school and studio run by a well-known painter; the best-known atelier was run by Charles Gleyre, where Bazille, Renoir, Monet, and Sisley met

baccalaureate   French school qualification, similar to a high school diploma

cataract   gradual misting of a lens of the eye, causing progressive loss of vision

classical   describes art that follows formal rules of construction and idealization rather than individual expression or truth

Cubism   art movement of the early twentieth century that abandoned notions of **perspective** and was recognized as one of the major turning points in western art. Although it was influenced by Cézanne, the artists most closely associated with Cubism are Georges Braque and Pablo Picasso.

Dadaism   violent, provocative, and anarchic art that mirrored the disillusionment many young artists felt with World War I

draftsmanship   technical ability to draw well

Dreyfus Affair   named after Alfred Dreyfus (1859–1935), a Jewish officer in the French army, who was wrongfully jailed for passing military secrets to the Germans. A campaign was started to have him freed and The Dreyfus Affair, as it became known, divided France. He was eventually found not guilty in 1906.

en plein air   painting in the open air to see colors in their true light

Expressionist   artist who abandons traditional ideas in favor of a style that exaggerates feelings or expressions. Van Gogh, an important forerunner of Expressionism, exaggerated nature "to express . . . man's terrible passions." Expressionist groups emerged in France and in Germany in the first decade of the twentieth century.

Fauvism   Expressionist style of painting inspired by the Neo-Impressionists and Cézanne, based on intense and vivid non-naturalistic colors. It emerged as the first major artistic development in the twentieth century. The leading artists were Henri Matisse and Paul Signac.

Franco-Prussian War (1870–1871)   war between Prussia and France that inflicted crushing defeats on France at Sedan, Metz, and the **Siege of Paris** and resulted in a humiliating peace at the Treaty of Frankfurt

Inquisition   Catholic organization established during the thirteenth century and surviving until the nineteenth century in Spain, designed to convince people who wanted church reform and nonbelievers that the Roman Catholic Church should be the most powerful faith

motif   dominant or distinctive figure or subject in an artistic composition

Neo-Impressionism   movement that grew out of Impressionism, fundamentally concerned with light and color but one based on scientific principles. Seurat, Signac, and Pissarro were its best-known artists.

Old Masters   term for art made from the 1400s until the 1800s by great artists of that time

palette   choice of colors of a particular artist or the actual board that an artist mixes his paints on while painting

Paris Commune   period of time in 1871 when Republicans controlled Paris. Defeat by Prussia left many unhappy with the French government. In March 1871, Parisian Republicans took control of Paris. French government troops entered Paris on May 21. The government and the Communards, also called Republicans, fought for a week. The Communards were cornered and massacred by the government troops, creating a tense political atmosphere in France.

perspective   method of representing space and depth on a flat surface

Pointillism   technique of painting using small dots of color instead of brushstrokes, so that when viewed from a distance, a bright and vibrant color mix is achieved. It is associated with the Neo-Impressionists.

Post-Impressionist   artist who followed the various trends in art that developed from, or in reaction to, Impressionism. Post-Impressionists include Cézanne, Gauguin, Seurat, Signac, and van Gogh.

retrospective   exhibition held to look back at an artist's career, to show the development of his or her work over time

Salon   annual exhibition of the French Royal Academy of Painting and Sculpture

Salon des Indépendents   exhibitions started in 1884 by Seurat and Signac in opposition to the official Salon

Salon des Refusés   exhibition ordered by Emperor Napoleon III and held in Paris in 1863 to show work that had been refused by the official Salon. Manet's *Luncheon on the Grass* was the centerpiece.

Siege of Paris   period of time during the **Franco-Prussian War** when Prussian soldiers surrounded Paris and would not allow any food into the city

Surrealism   art movement originating in France in the 1920s and characterized by the bizarre, dreamlike, irrational, and absurd

syphilis   serious sexually transmitted disease that can go into remission for many years before reinfecting the sufferer in a variety of different ways

Resources

List of famous works

Jean-Frédéric Bazille (1841–70)
Monet after his Accident at the Inn in Chailly, 1865, Musée d'Orsay, Paris
The Artist's Family on a Terrace near Montpellier, 1867, Musée d'Orsay, Paris
The Ramparts of Aigues-Mortes, 1867, National Gallery of Art, Washington, D.C.
Summer Scene, Bathers, 1869, Fogg Museum, Cambridge, MA
Studio in the Rue de la Condamine, 1870, Musée d'Orsay, Paris

Gustave Caillebotte (1848–94)
The Floor Strippers, 1875, Musée d'Orsay, Paris
Pont de l'Europe, 1876, Musée du Petit Palais, Geneva, Switzerland
Street in Paris, A Rainy Day, 1877, The Art Institute of Chicago, Chicago, IL
Self-Portrait, 1892, Musée d'Orsay, Paris

Mary Cassatt (1844–1926)
Woman and Child Driving, 1879, Philadelphia Museum of Art, Philadelphia, PA
Mother about to Wash her Sleepy Child, 1880, Los Angeles County Museum of Art, Los Angeles, CA
Lydia Crocheting in the Garden at Marly, 1880, Musée d'Orsay, Paris
A Woman in Black at the Opera, 1880, Museum of Fine Arts, Boston, MA
The Loge, 1882, National Gallery of Art, Washington D.C.
Children Playing on the Beach, 1884, National Gallery of Canada, Ottawa, Ontario

Paul Cézanne (1839–1906)
Dr. Gachet's House at Auvers, 1873, Musée d'Orsay, Paris
House of the Hanged Man, 1873, Musée d'Orsay, Paris
The Bay from L'Estaque, ca. 1886, The Art Institute of Chicago, Chicago, IL
Still Life with Apples, ca. 1890, The Hermitage, St. Petersburg, Russia
Large Bathers, 1895, The Barnes Foundation, Merion, PA
Monte Sainte- Victoire Seen from the Bibemus Quarry, 1897, Baltimore Museum of Art, Baltimore, MD

Edgar Degas (1834 –1917)
The Bellelli Family, 1860–62, Musée d'Orsay, Paris
Carriage at the Races, 1869, Museum of Fine Arts, Boston, MA
Woman Ironing, 1869, Neue Pinakothek, Munich, Germany
The Orchestra of the Opera, 1870, Musée d'Orsay, Paris
The Cotton Exchange in New Orleans, 1873, Fogg Museum, Cambridge, MA
The Ballet Rehearsal, 1873–74, Musée d'Orsay, Paris
The Dance Class, 1873–74, Musée d'Orsay, Paris
L'Absinthe, 1875–76, Musée d'Orsay, Paris
The Star, 1876–77, Musée d'Orsay, Paris
Miss La La at the Cirque Fernando, 1879, National Gallery, London
At the Milliners, 1882, Metropolitan Museum of Art, New York, NY
Ballet Scene, 1907, National Gallery of Art, Washington D.C.

Childe (Frederick) Hassam (1859–1935)
Rainy Day, Columbus Avenue, Boston, 1885, Toledo Museum of Art,
Toledo, OH
July 14 Rue Daunon, 1910, Metropolitan Museum of Art, New York, NY
Manhattan's Misty Sunset, 1911, Butler Institute of American Art,
Youngstown, OH
Fifth Avenue, April Morning 1917, 1917, Sheldon Memorial Art Gallery,
Lincoln, NE
Church at Gloucester, 1918, Metropolitan Museum of Art, New York, NY

Édouard Manet (1832–83)
The Spanish Guitar Player, 1861, Metropolitan Museum of Art, New York, NY
Luncheon on the Grass, 1863, Musée d'Orsay, Paris
Olympia, 1863, Musée d'Orsay, Paris
The Execution of Emperor Maximilian, 1868–69, Städtische Kunsthalle,
Mannheim, Germany
The Balcony, 1868–69, Musée d'Orsay, Paris
A Good Glass of Beer, 1873, Philadelphia Museum of Art, Philadelphia, PA
Repose: Portrait of Berthe Morisot, 1869–70, Rhode Island School of Design
Museum of Art, Providence, RI
Nana, 1877, Hamburger Kunsthalle, Hamburg, Germany
Bar at the Folies-Bergère, 1881–82, Courtauld Institute, London

Claude Monet (1840–1926)

La Terrasse à Sainte-Adresse, 1866, Metropolitan Museum of Art, New York , NY
Camille: Woman in the Green Dress, 1866, Kunsthalle Bremen, Germany
Women in the Garden, 1866–67, Musée d'Orsay, Paris
The Cradle – Camille with the Artist's Son, Jean, 1867, Musée d'Orsay, Paris
The Thames and the Houses of Parliament, 1871, National Gallery, London
Impression: Sunrise, 1873, Musée Marmottan, Paris
*Haystacks (series)*1890–91, Art Institute of Chicago, Chicago, IL, and Metropolitan Museum of Art, New York, NY
Monet's Garden: The Irises, 1900, Musée d'Orsay, Paris
Poplar Trees on the Epte River, 1891, Metropolitan Museum of Art, New York, NY
The West Front of Rouen Cathedral (series), 1892, examples in Metropolitan Museum of Art, New York, NY, and Musée d'Orsay, Paris
The Water Lilies, 1916–26, Orangerie, Musée National du Louvre, Paris

Berthe Morisot (1841–95)

The Mother and Sister of the Artist, 1870, National Gallery of Art, Washington D.C.
The Cradle, 1872, Musée d'Orsay, Paris
Young Woman in a Ball Gown, 1876, Musée d'Orsay, Paris
Summer, 1878, Musée Fabre, Montpellier, France
Eugène Manet and His Daughter at Bourgival, 1881, Private collection

Camille Pissarro (1830–1903)

Lower Norwood, London: Snow Effect, 1870, National Gallery, London
Lordship Lane Station, Dulwich, 1871, Courtauld Institute, London
The Red Roofs: Corner of the Village, Winter Effect, 1877, Musée d'Orsay, Paris
The Gleaners, 1889, Offentliche Kunstsammlung Kunstmuseum, Basel, Switzerland
The Rooftops of Old Rouen, Grey Weather, Toledo Museum of Art, Toledo, OH
The Place du Théâtre Français, 1898, Minneapolis Institute of Art, Minneapolis, MN

Maurice Brazil Prendergast (1859–1923)

Central Park 1901, 1901, Whitney Museum of American Art, New York, NY
The Promenade, 1913, Whitney Museum of American Art, New York, NY
Neponset Bay, 1914, Sheldon Memorial Art Gallery, Lincoln, NE
Salem Cove, 1916, National Gallery of Art, Washington, D.C.

Pierre-Auguste Renoir (1841–1919)

Lise with a Parasol, 1867, Museum Folkwang, Essen, Germany
La Grenouillère, 1869, National Museum, Stockholm, Sweden
Le Bal au Moulin de la Galette, 1876, Musée d'Orsay, Paris
Mme. Charpentier and Her Children, 1878, Metropolitan Museum of Art, New York, NY
Luncheon of the Boating Party, 1881, Phillips Collection, Washington D.C.
Washerwomen, 1888, Baltimore Museum of Art, Baltimore, MD
Young Girls at the Piano, 1892, Musée d'Orsay, Paris
Gabrielle and Jean, 1895, Musée de l'Orangerie, Paris

Alfred Sisley (1839–99)

The Square at Argentuil, 1872, Musée d'Orsay, Paris
Snow at Louveciennes, 1875, Courtauld Institute, London
Foggy Morning, Voisins, 1874, Musée d'Orsay, Paris
Floods at Port-Marly, 1876, Musée d'Orsay, Paris
Canal du Loing at Saint Mammes, 1885, Philadelphia Museum of Art, Philadelphia, PA

Where to see Impressionist art

France
Musée d'Orsay, Paris   **www.musee-orsay.fr**
This large collection of Impressionist art includes work by Monet, Manet, Bazille, Cézanne, Caillebotte, Degas, Renoir, Sisley, Morisot, and Pissarro.

Musée Marmottan, Paris   **www.marmottan.com**
This collection contains 65 paintings by Monet, plus works by Morisot, Pissarro, Renoir, Sisley, Boudin, Signac, and Manet.

U.S.
Art Institute of Chicago   **www.artic.edu/aic**
111 S. Michigan Ave., Chicago, IL 60603
(312) 443-3600
This collection has works by Bazille, Caillebotte, Cassatt, Cézanne, Degas, Manet, and Renoir.

Barnes Foundation   **www.barnesfoundation.org**
300 N. Latch's Lane, Merion, PA 19066
(610) 667-0290
This collection contains paintings by Cézanne, Degas, Manet, and Monet.

The Butler Institute of American Art
www.butlerart.com/collection/htm
524 Wick Ave., Youngstown, OH 44502
(330) 743-1711
This collection has works by American Impressionists, including Cassatt, Hassam, and Prendergast.

Los Angeles County Museum of Art   www.lacma.org
5905 Wilshire Blvd., Los Angeles, CA 90036
(323) 857-6000
The Impressionist works here include paintings by Cézanne, Degas, and Monet.

Metropolitan Museum of Art   www.metmuseum.org
1000 Fifth Ave., New York, NY 10028
(212) 535-7710
This collection includes works by Cassatt, Cézanne, Degas, Guillaumin, Manet, Monet, Morisot, Pissarro, Renoir, and Sisley.

Museum of Fine Arts, Boston   www.mfa.org
465 Huntington Ave., Boston, MA 02115
(617) 267-9300
The Museum of Fine Arts, Boston owns one of the largest collections of Impressionist works in the U.S. It includes 40 paintings by Monet, 20 by Renoir, 15 by Degas, and works by Manet, Sisley, Cézanne, Caillebotte, Guillaumin, Morisot, and Cassatt.

Museum of Modern Art   www.moma.org
11 W. 53rd St., New York, NY 10019
(212) 708-9400
This collection includes 22 Cézannes, plus pieces by Degas, Monet, and Renoir.

National Gallery of Art   www.nga.gov
Sixth St. and Constitution Ave., Washington, D.C. 20565
(202) 737-4215
This is another large collection of Impressionist art, including many Manets, and work by Cassatt, Degas, Cézanne, Morisot, Pissarro, Renoir, Bazille, Guillaumin, and Sisley.

Phillips Collection   www.phillipscollection.org
1600 21st St., Washington, D.C. 20009
(202) 387-2151
This museum owns paintings by Cézanne, Degas, Manet, Monet, and Renoir.

Further Reading

General Art Books

Brommer, Gerald F. *Discovering Art History.* Worcester, Mass.: Davis Publications, Inc., 1997.

Brommer, Gerald F. and Nancy Kline. *Exploring Painting.* Worcester, Mass.: Davis Publications, Inc., 1995.

Cumming, Robert. *Annotated Guides: Art.* New York: Dorling Kindersley Publishing, 1995.

Greenaway, Shirley. *Art: An A-Z Guide.* Danbury, Conn.: Franklin Watts, 2000.

Grovignon, Brigette. *The Beginner's Guide to Art.* New York: Harry N. Abrams, Inc., 1998.

Grolier Editorial Staff. *Looking at Art.* Danbury, Conn.: Grolier Educational Books, Inc., 1996.

Hollingsworth, Patricia. *Smart Art: Learning to Classify and Critique Art.* Tucson, Ariz.: Zephyr Press, 1998.

Mallory, Nancy. *European Art Since 1850.* New York: Facts on File Publishing, 1997.

Books about Impressionist Artists

Cassatt
Streissguth, Thomas. *Mary Cassatt: Portrait of an American Impressionist.* New York: Lerner Publishing Group, 1998.

Degas
Muhlberger, Richard. *What Makes a Degas a Degas?* New York: Penguin Putnam Books for Young Readers, 2002.

Mannering, Douglas. *Degas.* Broomall, Pa.: Chelsea House Publishers, 1997.

Manet
Chelsea House Publishing Staff. *Manet.* Broomall, Pa.: Chelsea House Publishers, 1997.

Monet
Muhlberger, Richard. *What Makes a Monet a Monet?* New York: Penguin Putnam Books for Young Readers, 2002.

Dorling Kindersley Publishing Staff. *Monet.* New York: Dorling Kindersley Publishers, Inc., 1999.

Index